The Next-to-Last American President

SHAWN O'REILLY

iUniverse, Inc.
Bloomington

The Next-to-Last American President

iUniverse books may be ordered through booksellers or by contacting:

iUniverse
1663 Liberty Drive
Bloomington, IN 47403
www.iuniverse.com
1-800-Authors (1-800-288-4677)

ISBN: 978-1-4502-9289-4 (pbk)
ISBN: 978-1-4502-9288-7 (cloth)
ISBN: 978-1-4502-9600-7 (ebk)

Library of Congress Control Number: 2011901496

Printed in the United States of America

iUniverse rev. date: 2/16/11

Foreword
by
Glenn Beck

Sorry, I could not contact Mr. Beck. His protective firewall is too high for an old fat man to climb. I mailed his organization a copy of this manuscript which they sent back unread. They were nice to send a kind letter and two bumper stickers.

I sent several people at "The Blaze" the manuscript by email. One lady did acknowledge she received it. That was the last response ever returned. I figured she was a liberal, overworked or crazier than Glenn.

Dear Glenn - You mention employing several Progressives. They could be like the French in WWII. You don't know if they are fighting with or against you. Most likely they are double agents, working both sides of the political spectrum.

I am a proud conservative, deeply worried if the United States will survive the next several years. This book describes a future date when the United States ceases to exist as a country. It details the downfall, aftermath and most important, the rebirth of the American People. Our country will recover from the impending economic, social and moral decay. The new governments and people will arise from the ashes of destruction and resemble more the intent of the original founding fathers. There shall be less regulation, taxation and infringement of government upon the God given rights of its citizens. The new motto: I eat, therefore I work.

A majority of the words and thoughts in this book were "lifted" from Great Conservative Radio and Television Personalities. It is not my fault: they speak and I must listen! My skull is an empty vessel ready to be filled with conservative Godly information.

Rush Limbaugh - The man who single handily started the Conservative Revival. Take care of your health! Your words of wisdom are needed more than ever. Live long and prosper!

Glen Beck - Always a bubbling fountain of required information. He and his advertisers gave many excellent ideas, which are written in this book. Those who listen to Glen will be better off in the days to come! Prophet of Truth to all that will listen.

Shawn Hannity - A true Reagan Conservative and all around nice guy. Please dump the Liberals on your show! I want nothing but the truth, the whole truth and nothing but the truth.

Phil Valentine and Johnny B - Entertaining and informative. A must for any afternoon of listening enjoyment. Phil had an early version of the manuscript hand delivered to his program manager at the radio station. Like many of the rich and famous, I was not worth a reply.

Mark Levine - A conservative pit bull. When he tears into a liberal, he never lets go.

In the beginning there was social justice throughout the land. Food was plentiful, there for the picking. Man lived in harmony with Nature having no fear or worries. Even the wild beasts were friendly. Climate changed as always without someone blaming Man. Clothing was optional since God placed them in a temperate earthy paradise and they knew no sin. Eve was in a utopia. There was no worry about wardrobe, shopping, cooking or housework. Dishes were not yet invented.

God told Adam and Eve to eat of all the fruit except that from the "Tree Of the knowledge of good and evil" in the center of the Garden. If you eat that fruit, you will be doomed to die. The downfall of the godly utopia began when Eve encountered a Progressive Snake in the grass. These creatures are to be avoided at all cost. The snake came to the woman and said "Really?" he asked. "None of the fruit in the garden? God says you mustn't eat any of it? "Of course we may eat it," the woman told him. It's only the fruit from the center of the garden that we mustn't eat it or even touch it, or we will die".

"That's a lie!" the serpent hissed." You'll not die" The talking snake convinced Eve to disobey God, eat of the forbidden fruit and give some to Adam. Eve believed the first lie that there are no absolute truths.

The serpent is with us, as from the beginning.

"If my daughters make a mistake, I don't want them to be burdened with a baby" The serpent hissed "YESSSS
"America is not a Christian Nation" YESSSS

"Yeah, I am a Christian, there are many paths to God" YESSSS

1

"No, No, No, not God Bless America, God____ America" YESSSS

Human life begins at conception! THAT'S A LIE!

After partaking of the forbidden fruit, Adam realized for the first time that Eve was naked. Soon they learned the purpose of each other's different anatomical parts.

In the beginning all was given by God. For this first sin of eating the forbidden fruit, God cast out Adam and Eve from the Garden of Eden. No longer would their every need be provided. They would survive by the sweat of their brow. They exchanged immortality in an earthly paradise for a taste of the forbidden fruit. Only a modern day Progressive would take that deal! If Eve had an earthly mother, she would have been warned about men, sex, and to stay clear of snakes, particularly the talking variety. Serpents like many politicians, speak with a forked tongue. Eve would also learn that men are interested in only one thing! (Peace and Quiet)

This dire outcome had to be the fault of someone, other than Adam and Eve. The progressive snake in the grass was nowhere to be found. After causing the first sin of Man it quietly slithered away. I did not know a snake could smile! Years later envy caused the sons of Eve to be pitted one against the other. The snake had another reason to gloat. YESSS

The Next To Last President

Barrack the next to last President
Had a contract out on U.S.
His Government took power
The people lost theirs
There is only so much liberty
Either for him or for us
Babies quiver in their mother's womb
Anxiously awaiting their turn
Grant him single payer health care
You will obey your master
The Free Market System is the only way
Of this I will never sway
"Never been proud of my country"
"Reparations don't go far enough"
Can he bankrupt US into prosperity?
Wake up; it's almost too late!

The United States of America has been morally, politically and financially in decline for many years. The mainline media, progressive professors and politicians controlled the ideological discourse and gained total control upon the people. Any one who contradicted their beliefs was discredited by any means possible. Because of their collusion, the truth about Progressives and the causes they supported could never be exposed. This led to the final chapter in the history of the United States of America with the Presidential Election of Barack Hussein Obama on November 2, 2008. The failure of the prior administration of President George W Bush left the country ripe for a political takeover. Bush's major lacking as President was the wasteful out of control spending and not securing and defending our southern border with Mexico. Mr. Bush was too "Presidential" to defend and properly explain his agenda to the American People. The Progressives and their media elite were more than happy to mention the errors of his ways. Without mounting a proper defense, the drumbeat of political opposition drove his approval numbers into the cellar.

Most Americans declare to be conservative on moral and fiscal issues. Old Blue Blood Country Club Republicans left Conservative Voters a poor choice in John McCain as our presidential candidate. The Democratic Candidate for President, Barack Obama, had easy pickings in defeating the Progressive Republican Candidate John McCain. If your choices for President are Progressive or Progressive-lite, why not go for the real deal. The rest of the story is unfortunately a sad one!

As a proud Conservative, "RINO" (Republican in name only) are now held in lower esteem than Progressives. At least you know that Progressives', however misguided have core beliefs. They blurred the political distinction between the Democratic Party and the Party of Lincoln. Moderate "RINO" Republicans like John McCain and Lindsey Graham led to the total political takeover of the federal government by the Progressives.

A RINO is a vague and despicable creature. It can never be trusted on what side of an issue it will support. It can turn against the conservatives at any moment. This traitorous action is most prevalent when manhood is most needed. "RINO" is a hideous creature in need of political extinction. It is best to excise them early in the primary season. A conservative is equal to two "Rino's". It takes two to equal one conservative since they only correctly vote fifty percent of the time.

I must admit voting for John McCain in the last presidential election. Being not pleased with the Republican Presidential Candidate, I had to close my eyes, hold my nose and pull the lever to register my vote. To summarize my feelings about this election, my bumper stickers read:

McCain

Palin

At least the lovely, talented and true conservative Sarah Palin was on the ticket. Her righteous balance was not enough to atone for progressive leaning Republican Presidential Candidate John McCain. He was at least the darling of the mainline media during the primaries. They supported a feeble republican candidate during the primary season to offer Barrack Hussein Obama a weak political opponent. Once the Republicans chose their Presidential Candidate, this ended the love affair with the Progressive media. Now they used all their biased power of the media to elect "The One". They enlisted comic imitators, not funny late night talk hosts, Holly weird Leftist, along with newspapers, magazines, unpopular radio shows and all television other than Fox. The Progressive Elite was stunned when John McCain picked Sarah Palin as his running mate. How could McCain betray them by picking a conservative woman? She must be personally and politically marginalized at all cost. Progressives in politics, media and other socialist groups convened a forum titled "Get Sarah". They saw only her as a political threat, and set forth a devious plot. Dear Sarah: As a southern neo gentleman, I will defend your honor! Sarah, a true woman, makes Hillary look very pale in comparison.

Thank God those mighty conservative warriors arose from the God Fearing, self reliant, taxpayer volunteers of the "TEA PARTY". The Tea Party is a bottom up, grass roots movement that brought a Conservative Revival. No longer will the Leaders of the Republican Party get away with producing a Progressive candidate for President. The Tea Party supports many great conservative women and men candidates. It is time for Conservative Women to ascend in political power. Sarah Palin is a positive role model for many as a wife, mother, and politician with her conservative, ethical and moral views. It has been recently mentioned that she is a one hundred percent natural woman. (No implants) Sarah's political support to a candidate is often a kiss of success. Her only political mistake was endorsing the re- election of John McCain. Because of that mistake, I have to lower her overall personal score to 95/100. When Sarah speaks, I watch and listen! Thank God for the legions of advancing conservative women like Michelle Bachman and Nikki Haley. Stay determined and on course, for you will be savagely attacked by progressives and their media elite. They will fabricate lies and speak against you will a single forked tongue.

Based on a Gallop survey March 26-28, 2010 showed that 37% of American Adults have a favorable opinion of the Tea Party Movement. Majority of Republicans (62 %) have a favorable opinion of the Tea Party, 37% of Independents and 14% of Democrats. Based upon the election results of November 2, 2010, more Independents are supporting the Tea Party Agenda. Tea Party Members are better educated and earn higher incomes than the overall voting population. The November 2010 midterm elections were a turning point in the resurgence of the Conservative Movement. This was the election that caused many progressive politicians to become ordinary citizens. I was pleased that Republicans once again gained control of the congress and held a majority of governors in the country. This election proved for all times that California is a land of "nuts and berries." The election of Jerry Brown as governor greatly accelerated the exodus of businesses and producers out of California. With the Republicans gaining the majority in the congress, "Nancy Pelosi, "the queen of San Francisco," lost her fleet of personal government aircraft along with unlimited extravagant food and drink. The sales of Jack Daniels plummeted after this election. Nancy was also at her best when she was a little "tipsy." The people of the country suffered mightily during the recession. Nevada led the way in those unemployed, number of bankruptcies, home repossessions, etc. I had sympathy for the people of Nevada until they re-elected "Dirty Harry'" November 2, 2010. Proverbs -"there's none as blind as those who will not see." For those who support corruption for their personal gain, the day of reckoning is at hand. This last statement also applies to the supporters of Barney Frank. I am ashamed of you! Always patrolling for rear, Barney has his sights set on the military, He has a "thing" about men in uniform. The Progressive's set forth new rules for gays in the military during the lame duck session in 2010. The new motto: Don't ask, don't smell, and give me some tail. This gives a new meaning of someone "watching your rear." The faithful question is have these miraculous political events of November 2, 2010, arrived too late to save the country.

Conservatives believe that power and liberty exist for the benefit of mankind. Government and taxation should be minimal. Progressives think that we exist to serve the government. There is finite supply of precious liberty. This Godly gift to America belongs with the people, not government.

A hundred years ago most people of all races were poor by today's standard. They were also honest, hardworking and God Fearing. People seemed to know and care more about their neighbors. When aid was needed, there were family, neighbors and the church. If a person was ill, neighbors would bring food, money and a doctor. Others would tend your farm until you were well. Every one who could was expected to work. You could leave your windows open and your doors unlocked. Life moved at a slower pace with less anticipation and stress. In many ways people were more satisfied and fulfilled. For their actions and beliefs in life, even with a meager existence, many have a mansion and want for nothing in Heaven. The importance of this life is largely to prepare for the next everlasting one.

As the Progressive Franklin Delano Roosevelt (FDR) accepted the 1932 Democratic nomination for president, he proclaimed, "Throughout the nation men and women, forgotten in the political philosophy of the Government, look to us here for guidance and for more equitable opportunity to share in the distribution of national wealth ... I pledge myself to a new deal for the American people. This is more than a political campaign. It is a call to arms." FDR assumed power rivaling that of a dictator. A good crisis should never go to waste! Recently Progressives have used the same thinking to forward their radical agenda. This was a time when many indigent people were forced to yield liberty to the Federal Government. To insure the support of the electorate, the populace must be made dependent on government for sustenance. Once liberty and freedom are traded, surrendered or stolen, it is almost impossible to regain. This is why the Progressives want as many Americans possible to be dependant upon their government. The trade for this dependency is more government control and votes for the Progressives. Most tyrants in history came to power during a depression or political upheaval when desperate people were grasping for a political or economic savior. The "New Deal" put Socialism on the fast track, attempting to "level the playing field" which later became "redistribute the wealth of the country to its rightful owners". This "New Deal" set into motion a progressive social disease that became the "Raw Deal" on America. This disease like leprosy started out as a minor infection that now has consumed man.

For over 50 years, European- Americans tried to make amends for the sins of past racial intolerance spending 5.5 trillion dollars on the failed War on Poverty. This program actually became the war on the American family, removing the financial and moral needs for many biological fathers to be no more than a sperm donor. The US national data handbook indicates that women having children out of God approved marriage continued to skyrocket to 40% of all births in 2010. In 1960 the total of out of wedlock births was 5% of the total births. As of 2010, the percentage of out of wedlock births was 28% for Whites, 51% for Latinos and 72% of all births by Blacks. This moral and social decay paralleled the decline of Judeo-Christian values. Children born out of wedlock are often a detriment to society, since they are more likely to commit crimes, fail in school, and be unemployed, morally deficient and dependent on government assistance. Some of these children by the grace of God, escape from the welfare state and become honest, productive members of society. They are the minority, but shows that one can escape the bounds of their environment. The circle of dependency must be broken, whatever the political, social and economic cost. If we as a country fail at this task, the end result will be the destruction of the country. Time for an economic reversal is dimming and without the painful remedy of massive spending cuts, the downfall will occur sooner and be more severe.

Many are trapped for life in the state of dependency. In essence, this is a captive "Taker" breeding program. Being subsidized for multi generational failure by the United States Government, the destructive pattern continued to grow. We have a perpetual generational maternally organized subset of society on welfare. This guarantees 95% of African Americans and 65% of Latinos being an indefinite voting block for the progressives to the end of government.

Sadly I believe the evolution and advancement of the human condition has stalled or is being reversed. In mans' past, if one was not productive, you had a nil chance of survival and passing on your genes. Today with the help of Progressives, this trend has been reversed. Compounding society's problems, the government subsidized Takers have a higher birth rate than the Producers. Thousands of years in the advancement of mankind are being threatened with the survival of the inept. Alpheus Hyatt stated "the theory of orthogenesis says certain trends, once started kept progressing even though they become detrimental and lead to extinction". I believe we are on that path!

Gratis dispensed from the Government started out as a trickle of the wealth of others and became a flood of red ink. This redistribution of wealth caused such elation among the Progressives and Takers, similar to a drug addict on crack. More and more wealth of others was required to maintain the high of moral superiority for the Progressives. The Takers demanded their Progressive Masters to redistribute more of the producer's earthly possessions. Spending withdrawal pains would be too horrible to mention! This uncontrollable government social spending grew into a present day financial flood, swamping the country in red ink. Even the innocent will not be spared from this disaster. Without government assistance, minorities will struggle more than others. This buying of votes using the wealth of the Producers became very expensive for all of America.

Lyndon Baines Johnson's Progressive War on Poverty morphed into the "War on the American Family." Government became the" eternal poverty pimp." This program makes the progressive heart swoon, but with most programs of its kind, is more grounded in emotion than reality. President LBJ and the word" War" is an American disaster story, whether the War on Poverty or the Vietnam War. At least the failure of the Vietnam War eventually came to an end. It must be added that the courageous US Soldiers were not at fault for the defeat in Vietnam. The defeat of both wars is squarely based on the incompetence of the civilian leadership. For years Presidents of both parties sent our soldiers to war and then restricted their ability to win. The latest example is Barack Obama's "don't fire until they shoot you first". Terrorist use our courageous solders for target practice. These terrorists are cowards, hiding under burkas and using civilians as human shields. One must kill the terrorist twice. First with a bullet, and then with a pig's foot inserted into some orifice.

The latest lame proposal is the "Military Medal for Courageous Restraint". It is a medal that service members can earn for doing nothing. I should have a closet full of those medals! Courageous restraint is where a soldier chooses not to use their weapon against a terrorist with his AK-47 ablaze, to save the life of a civilian. In summary - don't fire until fired upon and terrorist get a free hit when civilians are present. A good terrorist never goes into battle without civilians as a human shield. These terrorist are cowards hiding behind woman and children. To a certain extent, the military became an equal opportunity jobs program complete with affirmative action, and political correctness. Progressives disgusted by the thought of a righteous military took revenge upon the ranks. They pushed feminism, homosexuality, and the unfit into the military. If their people could not achieve the established physical, mental and moral standards, then the standards must be lowered or eliminated. Progressives openly professed how "they loathed the military". This Progressive dogma tainted many Generals and subordinates. Thank God that Afghanistan is the last major foreign military adventure of the United States of America.

Note - Please give the incompetent Wesley Clark another star! I forgot, thank God he and Colin Powell are retired.

It's Alive!

The Progressive elite leadership of the Democratic Party created the "Takers", people intentionality made to be totally and permanently dependent upon the Government. The Progressive Governing Elite look upon the "Takers" with disdain, objects only to serve their political whims. These elites consider themselves to be intellectually and culturally superior.

The following is part of an article by John Lillpop, October 20,2010 that appeared in the Canada Free Press: "Whackos at the Democratic National Committee (DNC) are supposedly convinced that both the House and the Senate can be salvaged by simply focusing on three important voting blocs known to be treasure coves for liberals. The Three voting groups that Democrats are counting to carry the day: - Illegal aliens Convicted felons, and The Dead

It is technically unlawfull for votes to be cast by, or on behalf of, a person in any of these categories. However, Democrat lawyers claim that laws that prohibit voting by illegal aliens, and convicted felons are discriminatory and unconstitutional." The Democrats can create voters as easy as the Federal Government can print money.

Illegal Immigrants and Takers were viewed all the same. Together they formed part of a massive Democratic voting block. Progressives attempted to reestablish the right to vote for convicted criminals. That would be one criminal voting for another! An illegal immigrant meant just another vote for the Progressives. This puts a new twist to "the more the merrier." Illegal

Immigrant's were a steady new source of voters. Climb the fence, cross the border and "the world is one's oyster".

The Progressives in Congress had begun a movement to add Puerto Rico as the Fifty First State. The majority of citizens in Puerto Rico would vote for the Progressives. This was part of a larger plot to have one party rule for eternity. Fair and honest elections would be a distant memory. "Thugs" of the Democratic Party Machine of Chicago ruled supremely over the common people of the United States. At the end of times progressive elites would regret the monster of dependency they fathered. This creature of dependency once unleashed would know no master! The progressives attempt to buy votes redistributing the wealth of producers, eventually put the country into an economic death spiral. They did not care whether the money was stolen, taxed or borrowed. Obama's desperate last words as President faded into the distance: "Mo Money, Mo Money, Mo Money, and Mo Money".

Times became so tedious and uncertain by January 2013; many found solace only with God. Conservatives prayed pleading for divine intervention. Wisdom, truth and justice only existed by the Grace of God. Jehovah responded with the sound of mighty trumpets saying: "I am the God of Abraham, ruler of all since the beginning of Time" " My God said further "You Progressive's have tainted the hearts of man and led them astray"! Government and nature is the false god's of many". "There shall be no worship of idols for I am the only and true God". Progressives went into shock over hearing the true words of God. They were led to believe there was no god other than the all knowing, all seeing Federal Government. A tree or Al Gore was never held with the same reverence by the environmental terrorist. Showing his anger, God turned the sacred Druid Forest into a large barren scorched mark upon the land. The Lord and Dark Prince of the Druids (Al Gore) was tried and found guilty of crimes against nature: enriching him while spreading the lies of Global Warming. He was caught lying on his back molesting another masseuse. Al's temperature and other things were caught while rising.

Global Warming hysteria morphed into climate change, since global temperatures were cooling. Espousing climate change meant the rants of Al Gore and other Greenie Weenies could never be disproved. Climate by its nature is always changing. He was sentenced by God to everlasting damnation and imprisoned by Man to the bowels of a dark and damp dungeon for the rest of his earthly days. His followers finally saw him as an environmental and moral harlot, but by then the destruction to the economy and country was beyond repair. Gore's gifted millions of dollars in stocks from goggle and other companies were now worthless as him.

The first wave of the economic tsunami that swamped the economy led to the Election of "The One, Barack Hussein Obama". This was set into motion with the infamous President Carter and the Housing Resolution Act of 1977. This Act in the name of social justice forced Banks and Mortgage Companies to give home loans without regard to the applicant's employment status, income, sanity or credit history. The ability to repay a loan should never be a factor for the financially impotent who in turn support the Democrats. President Bill Clinton put this sub-prime loan scheme on steroids. The recession of 2008 was largely due to the prior scheme of the Democrats. "A Government sponsored home loan for everyone is a vote for me". As all ideas from the Democrats, this venture was doomed to "crash and burn".

"Bubba" (Bill Clinton) was the best president the Chinese ever bought. Buddhist Monks in America, sworn to poverty and chastity, could each come up with $50,000 in cash for Clinton's campaign chest. Clinton however cordial with these Chinese Buddhist Monks had no concept of chastity. Cash from the Chinese Buddhist Monks sure beats Moses "Manna from Heaven". The Chinese ballistic missile program went from the Stone Age to the Space Age with "Bubba's" gift of top secret missile technology. May this missile technology never return to America carrying nuclear warheads?

Many Democrats professed that Bill Clinton was a Great President. This supports my assertion that the less done by the Federal Government, or President, the better. Bill Clintons view's on our enemies was "Terrorist, what Terrorist" as he moaned "O Monica". I thought underneath the desk of the President was a hiding place just for children. At least I think it was when JFK was in office. Monica should be given a medal for distracting "Bubba", keeping him from the peoples work. Otherwise, it is impossible to ascertain what other damage he might have done to the country.

The medal "courageous lack of any restraint" was given daily to Mr. Clinton.

Then Comes George

Most of Bill Clinton's shortcomings as president took several years to mature and blossom. George Bush's predecessor as President left festering problems that came to fruition during his time as President. These included the "No War on Terror", vetoing the drilling in the Artic National Wildlife Refuge (ANWR), and making the best coal reserves into a national park. Who knew we should actually fight the radical Muslim Terrorist? Why explore and develop our massive untapped natural resources? After all, oil could always be imported from the unstable Middle East. The benefits of abandoning your resources led to higher energy costs, unstable supply, high unemployment, budget deficits and providing financial support for Muslim Terrorists. We could always buy oil from Middle Eastern Countries who bankroll terrorist. This led to a massive transfer of our wealth to other countries. Many of these countries were hostile to the United States, but still would take our money. The billions of dollars leaving the country made a horrendous sucking sound. Progressives must at all cost appease the rabid Environmentalist and place our natural resources off-limits!

George Bush did raise concerns about the "Social Justice Home Loan Scheme." According to a Boston Globe article by Jeff Jacoby, September 28, 2008: "Affirmative-action policies trumped sound business practices". A manual issued by the Federal Reserve Bank of Boston advised mortgage lenders to disregard financial common sense. "Lack of credit history should not be seen as a negative factor ", the Fed's guidelines instructed. Lenders were directed to accept welfare payments and unemployment benefits as "valid income sources" to qualify for a mortgage. Failure to comply could mean a lawsuit". Mr. Jacoby wrote further that: "Barney Frank insisted that Fannie Mae and Freddie Mac were in good shape. Five years ago

(2003), for example, when the Bush administration proposed much tighter regulation of the two companies, Frank was adamant that "these two entities, Fannie Mae and Freddie Mac, are not facing any kind of financial crisis". When the White House warned of "systemic risk for our financial system" unless the mortgage giants were curbed, Frank complained that the administration was more concerned about financial safety than about housing.

Now that the bubble has burst and the "systemic risk" is apparent to all, Frank blithely declares: "The private sector got us into this mess."
Maybe George would have better results, but he was afraid to be in the same room alone with Barney. He broke out is a cold sweat even thinking about this scenario. How could he avoid his advances! I thought Texan's would not take crap from anyone. I forgot George was not a native Texan, just a northern transplant. Instead of wearing a "Ten Gallon" hat, he was allowed only the "Five Gallon" variety. Our current female conservative leaders show more manhood when supporting the values of the "Tea Party". The times are becoming so dire, that in order to survive we cannot compromise our conservative principles. This will be unpopular, but you will be vindicated in times to come. As a father, many decisions dealing with my children were not intended to make me popular. It will take them several years to appreciate my apparent wisdom.

The progressive leadership believed every citizen dependant upon the government should own a home, along with government provided food, cell phone, health care, retirement, fifty two weeks a year paid vacation, education and a "Bling" allowance. Barney Frank and Chris Dodd coddled and protected the sub-prime Ponzi scheme that finally collapsed the economy into a major recession in 2008. Barney Frank had an illicit love affair with "Fannie" Mae, which further clouded his thinking. I thought "Mae" was a women's name. The sub-prime loan scam was destined to fail. After all, it was just another government program. There is an old saying "Crap in, Crap out". The tidal wave of home loan defaults, spread over the country, causing economic devastation though out the land. This economic misery fermenting for years just happened to fall upon the latter years of the "W" administration.

The same politicians that caused the banking crisis were now in charge of fixing the problem. Many years before, a young Barack Obama sued

Citibank for having best and fair lending practices. Citibank used the same lending standards for all Americans, with race never being a factor. African Americans as a group had worst credit, lower income and less employment stability. This translates to fewer people in this group qualifying for home or auto loans. They overall had a higher home loan rejection rate or were forced to pay higher interest rates than the general population. If the numbers don't work out to your favor, it must be racism. Lord Obama told Citibank to make home loans to minorities regardless of credit, having a job, income, still in jail, or being deceased. Lawyer Obama worked with the nutty social justice at all cost group, Association of Community Organizations for Reform Now (Acorn). They forced Citibank into a large out of court settlement. Citibank relented to the blackmail from Obama. Otherwise, even though Citibank was innocent, they would be called racist for not submitting to the will of Obama. This racial bullying and blackmail served him well then and now as President. The government, Progressives, Acorn and others forced banks to participate in the sub-prime lending scheme. This eliminated many lending standards that had served the country well for years. Once the door for corruption was forced opened, it became a modern version of: "Bankers Gone Wild." Most hard working Americans were not a party to the sub prime government loan scam but greatly suffered during the long recession. Jobs were lost; wages and benefits were cut and value of their homes rapidly declined. As bad as the recession of 2008, few knew the worst was yet to come.

The "One"

Our young President, lacking moral and leadership experience other than a social agitator, was doomed from birth to fail as a leader of men. He was born of an atheist European-American mother and an African father steeped in revenge to level the playing field on a global level. Barack Obama's Grandfather "Hussein Onyango Obama "was arrested in 1949 and jailed for two years by the British in Kenya for subversive activities. This action created an intense racial hatred of whites, particularly the British in the Obama Family. This racial hatred was passed to Barack's father and later to our President. It must be in their African genes.

This resentment of the British is evident with Obama's interaction with BP during the gulf oil spill. He turned down the early request from Denmark and other countries offering to send specialized oil skimming equipment. By denying outside help, and impeding clean up actions by the State of Louisiana, he worsened the disaster. This way he could exact a greater price from the British Company. BP offered several plans to cap the flowing oil well to government regulators. BP suggested first plan A, to cut the casing and place a containment vessel over the wellhead. Plan A would initially allow more oil to flow into the Gulf of Mexico until the well was capped. So the Obama administration forced BP to use methods with a higher chance of failure. All the while oil was a flowing! Plan C failed and as plan B. Finally BP was allowed to implement Plan A, their first choice, and the well was capped. Is the government working for or against companies and the American People? This crisis empowered his kind to further regulate tax and limit the use of our natural resources. Never let a good crisis go to waste! The misery of others should always be used to further the Socialist Agenda!

Barrack's father became an expert on social justice, milking his blackness for every ounce of affirmative action and social promotion. The advancement of his cause was paramount, even at the expense of family and others. According to him, the evil European and European-Americans had stolen the natural resources of Africa, colonized the continent, and enslaved the population. The lack of progress in Africa had to be blamed on someone.

The senior Barack Obama abandoned his first wife and Barack Jr., when Barrack was only 2 years of age. Barrack's donor of sperm thought it was better to pursue his immoral convictions of social justice and need for racial revenge, than to be a father and husband. Besides, he could always find an ample supply of liberal like-minded white woman that would serve his every need. It was like buying a candy bar at the grocery store; if you run out, you can always get another one cheap! How could a good Muslim Man let his wife be seen in public without the head to toe covering? If Barack's mother would not either cover up or shut up, Barack Obama Sr. would have to leave. He also knew that gullible Americans would always provide for all the financial, physical and emotional needs of the young Barack. Since Barack was half African, it had to mean that his ancestors were mistreated and held as slaves years ago by the evil European-Americans. This terrible crime against nature had to be avenged! The shortcomings of the African race throughout the universe must be blamed and transferred to others. Barrack soon learned to dislike being of mixed race. He was having trouble even getting to first base with young impressionable female conservatives. Barack thought it must be his "Old Spice Cologne", not that he was damned at birth to be a Progressive, destined to destroy America and remake the country in his vision of Marxism. Barack seemed never to come to terms with being of mixed race. His mother often late at night would overhear the young Barack fussing at himself, "You Cracker", your N__ger. This would go on for hours at a time.

Baracks' favorite movie was "The Fly". This was about an eccentric European-American scientist who was working on teleportation. The scientist would be enclosed in an outgoing teleportation pod, his matter converted to energy and transmitted to the adjacent receiving pod where it was converted back to matter. If all worked out right, one might reappear in a form similar to what entered the first pod. A problem arose when a fly entered the teleportation pod as the scientist was energized. The genetic combination of man and insect was never meant, and a hideous creature was created. Young Barack was enthused with this concept: what if he had a device such as in the movie. He could go into the transmitting teleporter, be energized, and be transferred to the other pod. One night, while young Barack was fast asleep, dreaming of "The Fly"; he found himself, Karl Marx and Malcolm X all in the first pod. When the pod was energized and the transport was complete, what exited the second pod was a repugnant creature, only loved by progressives.

Barack was born somewhere, this we know to be true. For the sake of this story, let's say he was born in the state of Hawaii. The Hawaiian Islands were formed by a stationary mantle plum (hot spot) that the crust slowly moved over in the process of continental drift. The ancient indigenous people of Hawaii, not knowing they were over a geologic mantle plume, would make human sacrifices to the volcano gods, in an attempt to pacify the unknown power of the underworld. This seems like a waste of young beautiful virgins. What this has to do with Barack, I am not sure. Appeasement of dangerous people and natural events never work, and what a terrible waste of natural resources! Maybe a predecessor of Al Gore told the natives that the active volcanoes put out greenhouse gasses that would totally destroy the world and must be stopped at all cost. Why it is the leaders of any movement want lesser people to make the sacrifices for their cause?

Young Barrack's nickname was "Barry". When he was not going to the "Little Red Church" in Hawaii he loved to ride his bicycle. The only problem with bike riding is that there are hills to transverse. Barack would coast downhill and when he started climbing a hill and the pedaling became harder, he would call for his mother or others "to give a hand up". When a young friend asked him about this" Barack said he was entitled to help due to past racism of those evil European-American's." This was the infancy of his thinking that reparations will not go far enough to correct racial wrongs of many years ago.

Barack's mother Ann Dunham divorced his father for desertion and not being a Man. Ms Dunham later remarried another Muslim Lolo Soetoro and he moved the family to his home in Indonesia. In Dreams of My

Father, Obama states that during his time in Indonesia, his mother raised him to be contemptuous of America and Americans. Barack could only dream of his father, since he abandoned Barack at an early age. Maybe Barack dreamed if his life would be different if he had a father. The answers for many questions will never be fulfilled. Why had Barack's father abandoned him?

The dreams of Barack, his father and father's father once carried to fruition, became our socialist nightmare on Elm Street. This dream of Barack was most dangerous during his waking hours. As President, Baracks minions worked around the clock to implement his dastardly agenda. The country wished it could awake from his nightmare, but it was too late!
The gifts from Allah kept on giving.

It appears that the seeds for the ultimate revenge were firmly planted in the fertile Muslim soil of Indonesia. Obama lived in Indonesia from the impressionable ages of six to ten. He attended a Muslim School and became a regular fixture at a radical Mosque. A favorite course at this school was to "How to Defeat the Infidels. " Listed below is a copy of Obama's School notes on destroying the "Great Satan".

1. Force your enemy into financial oblivion with major budget deficits

2. Create a multi generational group totally dependent on the Government.
This Group known as the "Takers" will blindly support your Progressive Agenda.

3. Encourage open borders between the US and Mexico. Accuse any one against this as racist. A country without borders cannot survive.

4. Form a separate civilian defense force as large and well funded as the US Military. This is needed for any successful coup. You cannot trust the military leaders, particularly in the United States to turn against its citizens.

5. Islam says a Muslim can lie or verbally mislead the Infidels. Say or do anything that will give you the advantage. Allah is result oriented and will reward one with 70 virgins and a one-way ticket to their paradise.

The Muslim teachings and indoctrination would stay with Obama forever and be critical in his quest for power and glory. It was now clear the path needed for revenge. He must at all cost avenge his birthright and complete the jihad against the "Great and Little Satan" (US and Israel).

Young Barack was a daily fixture at the local mosque. Arriving early, he had his regular spot on the front row nearest to the presiding cleric. This way he could hear clearly the daily vitriolic sermons and never have to gaze upon the rear of another man. Also, since most worshippers bathed once weekly, it was better to keep your distance. He leaned forward towards the cleric as the words of Jihad filled the room. The cleric was most animated and spoke with authority when he preached "Death to the Jews, Death to Americans" Barry often recorded the cleric's words, playing them over and over until the words were firmly engraved in his mind and heart. His prayer rug being completely worn from wear had to be replaced monthly. Ms. Dunham fumed at her son for wearing out the knees of his trousers. It became such a problem that reinforced knee patches were required. The other Muslim children often made fun of Barack, calling him "patches". But young Barack was a favorite student in the eyes of the radical clerics. They saw he had great radical Muslim potential, and often would let young Obama lead the chants" Death to America, Death to Israel". The clerics knew that with their help, the boy would go far and be critical in defeating the enemies of Islam. The clerics now had an unholy instrument to destroy their enemies. With Barry, they would tame the "American Dog", and use American laws and kindness to destroy them. We must always show tolerance till our end! One would never wish to be called a bigot, intolerant or racist.

Some refer to Obama as a Manchurian Candidate, being a political figure planted and supported by our enemies. I don't know about Barry being a Manchurian Candidate. To be more precise, he was an Indonesia Candidate. From this point forward, the Indonesia Clerics sponsored and gave special Islamic training to Barack. He also received financial, immoral and other unholy support. It now seems the clerics have an excellent return on their investment, a gift that keeps on giving. Praise is to Allah!

On February 27th, 2007, Barack Hussein Obama said the Muslim call to prayer is "one of the prettiest sounds on Earth at sunset." In an interview with Nicholas Kristof, published in "The New York Times", Obama recited the Muslim call to prayer - the Adhan - with a first-class Arabic accent. He must take a daily refresher course!

The Adhan is as follows: (At the cost of one's soul, do not read out loud)

Allah is Most Great, Allah is Most Great
Allah is Most Great, Allah is Most Great
I bear witness that there is none worthy of being worshipped except Allah.
I bear witness that there is none worthy of being worshipped except Allah.
I bear witness that Muhammad is the apostle of Allah.
I bear witness that Muhammad is the apostle of Allah.
Come to prayer, Come to prayer
Come to Success. Come to Success.
Allah is Most Great. Allah is Most Great
There is none worthy of being worshipped except Allah.

The Islamic dogma is deeply engraved in Barrack's heart and mind. He knew the significance of these words from his Quranic Studies. A satanic aura surrounded "The One" as he earnestly spoke the words. Maybe this was the origin for many of their dark lord!

The Clerics remarked that Barack was their best student and future jihadist. After the cleric's instruction, he would be in the hands of Allah. They knew after he returned to Hawaii the American System of social justice, would further advance Barack with social promotion and affirmative action. Years later the Progressive Media would protect and shield their favorite son. The kindness of the American People will one day be their undoing.

Barack's High School Days

In 1971, Obama returned back to Hawaii to live with his liberal maternal grandparents, Madelyn and Stanley Dunham.

Barack's high schools days seem normal if you like to smoke marijuana, take cocaine, and drink yourself into oblivion. From Obama's (Bill Ayer's ghost written book?) "Dreams from My Father, suggest that he took marijuana and cocaine in part because of question his race presented. "I had learned not to care," he wrote. "I blew a few smoke rings, remembering those years Pot had helped and booze: maybe a little blow when you could afford it. Not smack, though." Sometimes he was so stoned, he didn't know what side he saw in the mirror. Since I am old and have never used drugs, I am unsure of what a "little Blow" really means. I looked up the word "smack", but the definition in Webster's Dictionary was not appropriate.

Obama's outlook on life would be different if his biological donor of sperm would have been a father. A caring and true God fearing father was needed to help the young Barack grow into manhood. The failure of males in society to act as fathers greatly damaged the social fiber that holds our society together. Perhaps if he had guidance of a just and loving father, his attitudes on race would be different. One must be content with their life, as it exists, to be truly happy in life. This fixation on race always dominated his thinking and outlook on life. Obama in the years to come continued to associate with others that would flame his hatred of America.

You would think Hawaii would have been a multi-cultural haven for the race obsessed Obama. Students of color were the majority in the school. European -American Students were the ones that were in the minority.

Obama should have flourished during his high school days since the racial tables were turned.

A disturbing pattern developed early in Obama's Life that he always associated with the "bad crowd." At Punahou High School he was a member in good standing of a "Pot till you Drop Club; otherwise known as the "Bingham Benches". He did hang out with athletes at school. They shared the common love of basketball.

An early mentor of Obama's in Hawaii was Frank Marshall Davis, an African American writer, poet and card carrying member of the Communist Party. He was a friend of Obama's maternal grandfather, Stanley Dunham who introduced him to Obama. Maya Soetoro-Ng, Obama's half sister, told the Associated Press that her grandfather had seen Mr. Davis was a "point of connection, abridge if you will, to the larger African-American experience for my brother". His grandfather would have done better to forget the hyphenated "crap" and concentrate on the American Experience for young Barack. This type of thinking only widens the racial discord, keeping us forever from coming together as "One nation, one people under God". According to the Enquirer, Barack was at the tender impressionable age of ten when he first met the family friend. For seven years he had a father son relationship with Davis, who has confessed to having sex with children, sadomasochism, bondage and practicing a wide array of deviant sexual activities. I am not suggesting that any inappropriate relationships existed between Barry and Mr. Davis. You could say that Barry had an interesting childhood.

In his memoirs, Mr. Obama recounts how he visited Mr. Davis on several occasions, apparently at junctures when he was grappling with racial issues, to seek his counsel. At one point in 1979 Mr. Davis described university as "an advanced degree in compromise" that was designed to keep blacks in their place. Mr. Obama quoted him as saying: "Leaving your race at the door. Leaving your people behind. Understand something, boy. You're not going to college to get educated. You're going there to get trained. He added," They'll yank on your chain and let you know that you may be a well-trained, well-paid nigger, but you're a nigger just the same".

Later in life he freely associated with the domestic terrorist William Ayers; convicted fundraiser Tony Rezko and his mentor Jeremiah A. Wright. This disturbing pattern of friends raises questions about Obama's lack of character. The question is: did Obama's influence morally corrupt others, or was he corrupted.

College Days

Obama attended Occidental College in Los Angeles for two years before transferring to Columbia in 1981. He graduated from Columbia in 1983 with a major in political science. Barack left such an impression of his time at Columbia, that few former classmates with the same major can remember him. It is known Obama lived off-campus with a Pakistani roommate identified as "Sadik," who was a Columbia student. Obama describes Sadik "as short, well-built Pakistani" who smoked marijuana and snorted cocaine. Sadik's real name was really Sahole Saddiqui. Sahole was an excellent roommate for Obama in many ways, since sharing so much in common. "We were both very Lost," Sahole told AP (Associated Pravda) of his days in New York with Obama. "We were both alienated, although he might not put it that way. Sahole and Barack were such good friends that they often used each other's prayer rugs and bongs. Barack did complain that Sahoe's rug often smelt of curry. (Joke)

After graduating from Columbia, Obama spent four years as head agitator in chief working with socially disturbed African Americans on the south side of Chicago. He could never understand that his hard work never made a real or lasting difference. After this gig, Barack moved on to Harvard. The Indonesia clerics in his past were overjoyed that he was socially promoted to Editor and Chief of the Harvard law Review. He had a racial overtone, Mr. Obama said; "I personally am interested in pushing a strong minority perspective, I'm fairly opinionated about this. But as president of the law review, I have a limited role as only first among equals."

After graduating from Harvard he worked as a civil right's attorney in Chicago. During this time while associated with Acorn, he cried Racism and forced Citibank into a large out of court settlement. He had a part early on in "giving anyone a home loan" plan. This plan was later known as the sub-prime lending scam, leading to the worst recession in 70 years. He was a member of the Illinois State Senate from 1997 to 2004. During that time Obama voted for "killing the fetuses twice act". If a baby survived a botched abortion, withhold medical aid and let it die. He expressed a similar attitude later," If my daughters make a mistake, I don't want them burdened with a baby". My spin - If the country makes a mistake, I don't want them burdened with a Barack Hussein Obama. Barack is a historic transmutation figure determined to remake the world is his ideological image.

There were visible cracks in the aura allowing a glimpse into his real nature. The true lack of character was clear for all to see. A few looked into the light and saw the truth! Some looked but would not see! Many others warmed by his glow, didn't care about truth or the source of his brilliance. Most in the media coddled his candidacy defending and denying his radical agenda. They insulated the public from the truth of his collusion with Jeremiah Wright. Chris Matthews after Obama gave him a tingle down his leg said "I want to do everything I can to make this thing work; this new President work". Note to Chris: Making Obama succeed in turn means the demise of the country. Chris looks pretty sick in an Obama girl cheerleader outfit. His outlook on life is paler that his legs. He will one day know the folly of his thinking in this life or the next one. Will Satan need a commentator to carry his propaganda? A tingle down your leg there might mean a body part on fire, or the arrival of Barney Frank.

The people of Illinois elected Obama to the United States Senate, where he served from January 2005 to November 2, 2010. His presidential campaign began in February 2007. Now he was close to completing his final revenge.

RV Wright Days

At first thinking this section would be my favorite part. As it progressed, I became very sad. The negative influence on others including our President makes Jeremiah Wright a pivotal negative personality in my lifetime. From Jeremiah came the ascension of the "One. Listening and incorporating the racist and black liberation rants of Jeremiah, helped make Obama the man he is today! Jeremiah's beliefs are due to being a Muslim, Marxism, and Black Liberation Theologian with a pinch of Christianity. Now that is messed up! This radical thinking is the same as his disciple Barack Hussein Obama. The acorn does not fall far from the tree. The dash of Christianity helps make the gooney gook go down. They fit the definition of "being all things, to all men". This way if queried about your religious belief, you can be almost anything in your mind. Sadly, Christianity doesn't belong with that nonsense. The bottom line analysis is that they believe in hatred toward those who are different. This includes skin color, followers of the constitution, freedom and the "Little and Great Satan". After all, their main goal in life is racial revenge. That is why reparations could never be enough. They must make their enemies pay, pay and pay. Even after death, they will still blame you for being white, a capitalist or Jewish. I wondered earlier why they hated the Jewish People. Being a Christian I have historic religious affiliation with the Jewish People, particularity in Israel. Then I realized that Jeremiah and Barack are not Christians.

Never have I heard or seen a more colorful person as Jeremiah Wright. I cannot refer to him as Reverend, since this association would forever tarnish Christianity. My Lord Jesus Christ many years ago climbed the steps and knocked on the front door of The Trinity United Church of

Christ in Chicago. Jeremiah Wright slowly opened the massive wooden door and in disbelief for seeing "Jesus" at his church said" Hell No, not in my house "and slammed the door. Jesus had not been welcomed there for many years. When I heard this, I had empathy for my Lord. He freely offered salvation, but many would not accept this eternal gift, bought and paid for with his most precious blood. It is a terrible spiritual crime the thousands including the Obamas', Jeremiah led astray.

Jeremiah Wright's Top Sermon Titles

1. Whites not Right!
2. Them Jew's got my money
3. Live for today, hell with tomorrow
4. Them chicken's are a roosting
5. Jeremiah's in the House
6. Jesus Who?
7. No cash, take EBT Cards
8. Follow me to the "Promised Land"
9. It ain't my damm fault
10. Yos yer Daddy, don't ask yer Momma

Wright's comment on God and government:

"And the United States of America government, when it came to treating her citizens of Indian descent fairly, she failed. She put them on reservations. When it came to treating her citizens of Japanese descent fairly, she failed. She put them in internment prison camps. When it came to treating her citizens of African descent fairly, America failed. She put them in chains, the government put them in slave quarters, put them on auction blocks, put them in cotton field, put them in inferior schools, put them in substandard housing, put them in scientific experiments, put them in the lowest paying job, put them outside the equal protection of the law, kept them out of their racist bastions of higher education and locked them into positions of hopelessness and helplessness. The government gives them the drugs, builds bigger prisons, passes a three-strike law and then wants us to sing 'God Bless America." No, no, no, not God Bless America - that's in the Bible -- for killing innocent people. God damn America, for treating our citizens as less than human. Goddamn America, as long as she tries to act like she is God, and she is supreme. The United States government has failed the vast majority of her citizens of African descent."

My comments:

America was a great and generous country. It is comprised of men and women who sin and fall short of the expectations of God. Our country has worked towards addressing past racial transgressions using affirmative action, social promotion and cradle to grave welfare. The outcome of over fifty year's effort, spending twelve trillion dollars on the "War on Poverty" has been a dismal failure. We have created nothing but a multigenerational welfare state. The problem, Mr. Wright, is that you spend all your efforts living in the past, creating and fostering racial hatred. The many years of Affirmation Action, Social Promotion, and cradle to grave welfare state made no difference in the percentage of the population who are considered "poor". Mr. Wright, you and other like-minded socialists instead of encouraging 'people to be the best they can be', blame your shortcomings and lack of success on others. You have committed the worst sin of all, telling the youth not to strive for excellence, since "Whitey" will not let you succeed. This philosophy of revenge and being victims due to race has caused many not to strive and achieve the American Dream. Instead they expect and demand the Federal Government provide their earthly needs. It is better to be a fundamentalist, regardless of wealth and station in life and later have an eternal mansion in Heaven. A short Godly life lacking material wealth is greatly superior to living a thousand years with wealth and power as an agent for Lucifer. Mr. Wright has greatly failed as a minister for God, but is Satan's superstar. It will be easier for a camel to pass thought an eye of a needle, than he and his parishioners to make it to heaven. They regularly attended church, wore their finest Sunday clothes and heard the Black Liberation rants of a racist madman. They did go to church, the wrong one!

Barack and Jeremiah became close friends during their over 20 year association. Jeremiah married Barack and Michelle at the temple of Black Liberation. That was an interesting ceremony! They often would visit each others home. On one visit to the Obama's, Barack showed his prize collection of prayer rugs. His must admired object was a sword said to once belong to a general in Saladin's Moslem Army. The sword dated from the crusades, and was said to have removed the heads of many captured Christ Templar's. The Templar's once captured were always executed since they would never convert to Islam. To a radical Muslim and follower and leader of black liberation theology this had great significance. The templar's were both white and Christian.

At Jeremiahs mansion in a gated community, he showed Barack all his African artwork and sculptures. The most imposing item was a six foot tall statue of a muscular black arm with clinched fist reaching towards Mecca. The most disturbing item was a painting of a half black man fighting against his white self. The meaning of this painting was only known by Barack and Jeremiah. I saw a photo of the painting. It reminded me of a scene from Hell where a man is greatly tormented.

The Trinity United Church of Christ was Barack Obama's meeting place in Chicago for Black Liberation Indoctrination for over twenty years. In the minds of many African Americans, Christianity was long associated with slavery and segregation. It breaks my godly heart to even write this nonsense. My comment is it was not Christianity, but those that did evil in the name of Christ. Christianity is based upon faith, not social status. It saddens me most that the Lucifer Black Liberation Movement has led many astray, leading them on a path towards eternal damnation. On judgment day, Jeremiah Wright will stoke the fires hotter than normal. After dying, Jeremiah awakes to the afterlife and says, "Where the hell am I".

Black Liberation Theology views Christianity only as a means to support Black Liberation in the present, and minimize the more important eternal afterlife. Don't they know this short life is preparation for eternal life to come! I have hope in Jesus, the Son of God, who willingly died on the cross, sacrificing his life to forgive my sins, that I shall have eternal life. When Barack was asked if he was a Christian, he said, "yea, but there are many paths to God". His definition of a Christian does not compute. He and the other Black Liberationist's must be reading the Louis Farrakhan's version of the Bible. Louis Farrakhan is a radical Muslim American leader who is another anti- European American, Anti-American and Anti-Semitic Racist of the fourth order. I now understand why Farrakhan received a lifetime achievement award from "The Trinity United Church of Christ". For most practical purposes, Wright and Farrakhan are identical as "Racists" haters of America. Why are the mortal crimes of these individuals never exposed by the old main line media? This explains how many African Americans seem to have a lingering resentment or hatred of whites. If you cannot forgive, how can you expect to be forgiven! My one and only true God, tells me that I should never judge a person by their skin color, or for any other trait that is beyond their control. My niece, Megan added, "Born out of wedlock is "Beyond their control". She was referring to children, not their parents. It was as if I was placing blame on an innocent newborn.

Dear Megan: the children borne out of wedlock, or thru God approved marriage are innocent of the sins and deeds of others. It is important that children don't repeat the mistakes of their biological parents. The cycle of poverty, government dependence, and out of wedlock births should be discouraged. In this case, may the circle be broken. Children are born with a blank slate; shaped by environment, society and heredity. If one expects society to satisfy earthly needs, then society is obligated to establish guidelines for behavior.

If biological parents lived and cared first and foremost what was best for their children, they would make fewer mistakes in life. Important decisions should be made with guidance from God, and what is best for their children.

The Black Liberations' believe God will lead only blacks to the Promised Land. Don't they know they are already here! America was once a land of milk and honey, a shining beacon of light spreading justice, freedom and opportunity throughout the land. In the Exodus, God led Moses and the Israelites from Egypt as slaves to the "Promised Land". The Jews were led to a place of 'milk and honey". Unlike the Black Liberationist, they knew that only hard work would milk flow and honey had to be found and collected. They are destroying their "promised land" by many being a "Taker" and their misguided unduly political support of the Progressives. "Being Christian does not mean following in his (Jesus) steps". (Black Theology and Black POWER, PAGE 139(3). If African American's who descended from slaves had a choice, would they rather live here or in the dark Sahara? Let's check our immigration records of American's moving to Africa.

Apparently some black religious leaders preach sermons more about white racism, than on God. Their congregations will be well versed on the racist evil actions of Europeans and European Americans and how they continued to be mistreated, but gain little knowledge of CHRIST! In Jamaica 'Man" they blend together Christianity and Voo Doo. Voo Doo is carried over from their days in Africa. Jamaica college students go to Voo-Doo U. This is similar to the African Descendents in American combining Black Liberation Theology with a dash of Christianity. This must be an "African Thing". Unfortunately this will be useless when you leave this world, and your deeds are revealed in the "Book of Life". God upon reviewing your life will say" You did not know me in life; I do not know you in death." Jeremiah Wright for the first time was turned away. Affirmative Action, Political Correctness and Social Promotion had finally failed him.

A similar mixing of beliefs has occurred in many churches of white folk. The Progressives added their ungodly magic, turning many former houses of God into a temple for Social Justice. My Lord was once the focus of their worship. He has been dismissed and demoted to the bottom of many churches list of priorities. Social Justice is always at the top of the list. This makes the congregation feel very good about them. A Progressive Minister must feel very self-righteous. They cannot hide in their robes from God. He knows who and what you are! I faced my Lord seeing he was very distraught! A tear flowed down his cheek and he said "Did I Die for nothing"! My heart broke upon hearing his words. I fell to my knees and wept.

A long time thinking that many things in common with African Americans and others of different political persuasion was the common belief in "Christ". It was a sad day when finding that the "Christ" of many is not the one I love and trust.

Victor Hansen wrote "Obama, by what he wrote in his memoirs, by what he said when he spoke in his early campaign speeches, by his frequent praise of Wright, and by his 20 years presence in front of, and subsidies to, Obama knew exactly the racist and anti-American nature of this odious pastor. Fox News' Bill O'Reilly said of Wright, "In my opinion, RV. Jeremiah Wright is not an honest man. He preaches anti-white (European American) and anti-American rhetoric, all the while making money of it." A great African American economist and commentator Thomas Sowell wrote that there was" no way that (Obama) didn't know about Jeremiah Wright's anti - American and racist diatribes from the pulpit." He wrote that Obama was "no Ordinary Member" of the church, having once donated $20,000 to it, and Obama's speech was "like the Soviet show trials during their 1930s purges', intended only to convince supporters.

Barack, I know you to be a very intelligent person! Your memory must either be faulty, or you are a liar, if you never heard the racist and anti-American rants of Jeremiah. The problem is you heard the words and the words became you! Fugue - A pathological condition during which one is apparently conscious of one's actions but has no recollection of them after returning to a normal state (Webster's II). Maybe Jeremiah's hypnotic rants put his congregation into a trance. They return to normal after passing the offering plate. This way they cannot remember what happen to their EBT Card, liquor fund or life savings. This allows Jeremiah to live the high-life. The excuse of not hearing what was said, only works with me dealing with my wife!

The nut job President of Iran, Ah mad in ejd thinks by causing mass destruction and turmoil on earth it will foster the return of the twelfth Imam. This Imam after rising out of a well will cure all the ills and problems on earth. It would be like a Moslem fairyland. The leaders of Iran reason that losing seven million of their countrymen is a good outcome to vaporize seven million Jews. Ah mad thinks that is a fair trade. Hey, we have seventy million, they have seven million. Losing one Iranian to kill one Jew is no problem! On a one to one comparison, Ah mad has plenty of Iranians to spare.

The nut job President of America, Ba rack O bama thinks in a similar fashion. Causing economic and moral destruction of America, an era of Progressive enlightenment will also arise from the ashes. This would be a Progressive fairyland.

Ah mad's savior will come from the ground, mine will descend from Heaven. That's all that needs to be said!

Barack's steals money from the American People to build/remodel mosques throughout the Moslem world. In return the Moslems persecute and murder Christians because there is no tolerance in Islam. What Muslims did not convert by the sword, they now will conquer by immigration and a high birth rate. Europe, Oh Europe, how gullible are you! You allowed the enemy freely into your mist. America, Oh America, how gullible are you! They will build their mosques, increase in population and one day destroy the country that showed them great kindness and tolerance. Allah says thanks for the welfare. His people live well in America and Europe.

In Islam if the infidels want convert you can:

1. Kill them
2. Enslave them
3. Confiscate their wealth through exorbitant taxation. Obama has initiated   this part first, the day after inauguration. This action was done under the pretext of "Social Justice".

Cartoon - During the crusades Saladin and his Muslim forces are attacking a Christian Crusader Castle. Barack in his former life is inside the castle. He opens the castle gates clearing the way for the Muslim hordes. A Christ Templar fighting for his life cries out his last words to Barack "I thought you were a Christian"

Nothing Lasts Forever

Americans inherited many sacred gifts. These included our constitution, stable republic form of government, sacrifices of our forefathers and wisdom by the grace of God. At the end the gifts from our founding fathers and God were squandered as throwing "pearls to the Swine".

Barack and Michelle felt entitled by birth and this was acerbated by their status as President and First lady. Now for the first time nothing was beyond their reach. If Michelle is the First Lady, who was Number Two? They behaved and spent our money like they were King and Queen and the country belonged to them. Michelle flew into a rage at the end of their reign, being told she could not take another lavish tax payer journey to Spain. Michelle modeled herself after and emulated Marie Antoinette. She would often come out of the White House closet, wearing a seventeen century style flowing gown. Her ruby slippers had real rubies. Even the secret service was forced to bow before her person. The growing number of hungry, unemployed citizens resented their flaunting of our former wealth and their supposed superiority. Queen Michele saw the ending of their reign, and hoped to avoid the fate of Marie.

The date is October 4, 2012. The bow of the ship of state slipped beneath the waves of discontent. United States of America became a moral and economic wasteland. The unemployment rate is so high that the number was no longer relevant. The government's accumulated debt peaked at 21 trillion dollars. The economic tipping point was when the interest on the national debt exceeded all tax receipts. It's difficult to tax a man with no job or income. Government bonds and treasury bills had moved far past the level of junk bonds. Before these financial instruments became worthless, Uncle Sam was offering sixty nine percent rate of return annually on Treasury Bills. No one or country in their right mind would loan money to the US at any interest rate. Some Progressives in their left mind still had hope for "Social Justice".

For some time the Progressives believed conditions were trending in their favor. Their cold hearts were overjoyed with the election of the "One". Progressives were masters on getting a return on their political investment. They could swap billions of borrowed or stolen dollars of the people's wealth to support the union bosses, who in turn would give them millions in political payback and send hordes of the living, near death and dead to vote for the Progressives. Election day for Democrats reminds one of the movie" Weekend at Bernie's". I hope to be that active when I am dead! Bernie votes for Democratic candidates at every election.

Chrysler and GM (government motors) will not change their union dominated ways and will eventually go the way of the dodo. A new Chevy Impala actually cost fifty thousand dollars. That breaks down to twenty five thousand for the sales price of the vehicle and twenty five thousand per vehicle for the Union Bosses. What a deal for the taxpayers! Was this the "New Math" of the socialists? What's even better, it's done all with borrowed money. Our grandchildren will be forced to pay for extinct auto companies and their union bosses. I can imagine a young child many years from now asking his grandfather "what is a GM". The grandfather replies "one of many costly mistakes for you to pay". Too many living for the moment is all that matters. Would this Progressive-Union Bosses affair continue without extortion money stolen from the taxpayers?

In 2010 Obama nominated Elena Kagan and she was confirmed as a new associate justice of the Supreme Court. The prior year he nominated Sonia Sotomayor. With these two new Progressive Supreme Court Justices, forty five percent of the justices did not believe in the original intent and meaning of the Constitution. This old piece of paper was just a hindrance to their ambitions. May 2011 was another turning point in the history of American justice. A conservative Supreme Court Justice, seeing how Obama decimated and trashed his beloved constitution had a fatal heart attack. President Obama even with the impending doom knew he had a historic opportunity to appoint one more Justice. Never again would there be a five to four decision against his agenda. He nominated Rashad Al Khomeini as the last Supreme Court Justice. The votes of all the Democrats and one Republican Senator confirmed Al Khomeini. At that moment the court was neither just nor supreme. Many people already panicked by the downward economy and the inept leadership of the federal government lost all hope, and took to the streets. This was not "The Change" many had given their support and vote.

The stock market had completely tanked. Berkshire Hathaway INC DEL stock price was $116,455 per share June 16 2010. By the end of 2012 the stock price was $11.6455. This price was outstanding compared to other stocks. The "Oracle of Omaha" Warren Buffett had worked his financial magic once again. Berkshire Hathaway Company Geico was forced into bankruptcy. Geico tried to continue paying its employees with worthless dollars. All premiums and claims paid were also paid in dollars. This financial charade could not last! The Geico Gecko was given a pink slip joining the millions now unemployed. He was last seen leaving town on foot with his entire Gecko earthly goods wrapped in a tiny bag at the end of a small twig, hung over his right shoulder. He traveled only during the day, since Owls patrolled the night's sky. At least he was lucky that no clothes were required. He was heading back to the home country. Geico's advertising stated his origin was England, New Zealand or Australia. It couldn't be Australia, since he is not a marsupial. A pouch would be handy for storage.

Unfortunately most of the richest people in the world wealth were invested in financial instruments tied to the dollar. They mastered and controlled vast quantities of stocks, bonds, and certificate's of deposit, savings accounts and much more. Most of these investments now were not worth the value of their paper. The economic collapse was harder on the former rich. They had more assets to lose and further to fall down the economic ladder. Since many wealthy people in New York lived in exclusive top floor penthouses, they made a greater splash when jumping through windows.

All those who participated in the selling and buying of carbon offsets, lost everything. This hoax exposed many as harlots in the environmental movement. Al Gore had greatly enriched himself while being the pied piper of the green movement. Greenies would blindly follow their Druid Priest as he led them over a cliff. Under that scenario, at least Al would go first. Many investors seeking revenge for financial losses forced Al Gore into hiding. Luckily for him he had many mansions, constantly moving to keep his seekers confused. Later he was caught, tried, convicted and given a new home.

If only these people had listened and obeyed Glen Beck and heeded the advice of his commercial sponsors. They would have ample supplies of gold, silver and a year's supply of survival food and non-hybrid seeds to grow one-acre survival garden. Many scoffed at the words of Glen Beck, only to realize too late their folly. A Prophet is seldom appreciated during his lifetime.

As the economy collapsed, higher and higher interest rates were offered by the government to sell their junk bonds. This futile effort lasted three weeks, before the president ran out of all options. He tried to confiscate all personal savings and monies in retirement plans. Obama would issue IOU'S stamped with his personal seal. Even the normally supportive progressive RINO Senators Collins and Snow would not submit to this idea. I bet they were easy in their younger days.

 No one would ever buy Treasury Bills or bonds. He tried to quell the rage of the citizens, blaming the economic downfall on the banking system, Bush and Capitalism. Obama believed that he and his words were meant for others to hear and obey. His words became nothing more than mindless chatter, a mistake that took his followers several years to realize. Words became as hollow as the stomachs of many Americans.

The Obama Administration would never limit the growth of the entitlement and welfare state, spending US into oblivion. He made the socialist European Counties seem conservative by comparison. Barack fell into a deep state of depression. Government had always existed to serve him and his kind. He was the President of the United States of America, once the most powerful man in the world. Citizens needed his supreme progressive wisdom to guide them through perilous times. Since he was intellectually and morally superior, lesser people needed to follow his commands. They, like young dependant children do not know what is best.

The Progressives even lost support of the 'AP" Associated Press and the "AM" Associated Media of ABC. NBC, CBS, CNBC, NPR and CNN.

News Anchors and senior reporters of the "AP" and "AM" awoke early each morning anxiously awaiting their daily talking points from their Leftist comrades in the Democratic Party. Every day they repeated with glee the same message taken from their talking points. They either were mindless news zombies, or totally in the tank with the Liberals. Who wrote the words that they repeated? Their message was so homogeneous, that it had to originate from one source. This control and leftist slanting of the news and opinion furthered the demise of the country. Why would the population be swayed by the agenda of the Left? It had to be by lies and deceit. Towards the end, the leftist elite media became politically disturbed that they lost control of the message. August 22, 2010 I watched a pathetic segment on the CBS Morning Show. A bitter old man was reporting how terrible that blogs on the internet were reporting truthfully that Barack is a Moslem. You could feel the anger extruding from his beady eyes, wrinkled face and monotone voice. He privately was devastated that the "AM" and "AP" had lost the monopoly on controlling the propaganda. His last broadcast words were Damn the internet, Damn Fox News. At the end, no media remained to spread the propaganda of the "left".

Many realized too late that the only unbiased media was Fox, Conservative talk radio and the Enquirer. The beacon of Journalism, the National Enquirer was the only source both to break the John Edwards and Barack Obama marital infidelity stories." Now that had to be hard news". Katie Couric always last in the ratings now sat alone in her anchor chair. She now had just two viewers, both relatives. The studio lights faded to black.

My thoughts about the Associated Press

Associated DE-Press-ed

Their works are black on white
All I see is Red!
Why even read it
To get depressed
They are so slanted
Left and backwards
Their Progressive Ideas
Destroy man's will
Motives dark and dangerous
Hidden mostly out of sight
Need the "doctrine of fairness"
Their ideas can't compete
They call you many names
Don't be afraid
Be sure your heart is true
That will make them blue
Shine the spotlight of truth
Watch them slither slowly away

Barack thought back to his childhood days in Indonesia. Finding notes from his favorite course" How to defeat the Infidels" he remarked that he followed faithfully the teachings of his favorite cleric Matada Duballa Alli Wenki. He had believed every word, where had he gone wrong! Could it be that he trusted in the wrong Deity? Every step of his notes was faithfully followed, except there was not time to fully implement the "Obama Civic Defense Force, OCDF ". With the social justice mobs and Takers raiding the White House, running off with large screen televisions, Kobe Steaks, Michelle's "Bling" and everything else, the Obama's huddled alone in the secure basement bunker of the former White House. He knew too late, that he should have fully implemented the "OCDF", before taking over health care.

The Progressive's had earlier tried to right the crumbling economy by raising taxes. The upper income federal tax rates were at 95 percent, but no amount of taxation could right the financial ship. They were incapable of making the hard decision to reduce government spending. Dirty Harry introduced the VAT (Value Added Tax) in January 2011. The VAT placed a tax on every level of production. It in essence was a national sales tax. The value of the dollar plummeted on the worlds market, sending the world into a depression of biblical proportion, never seen in the short history of mankind. Pelosi's face fell as the nation's economy collapsed. Obama ordered the treasury to print currency around the clock, thinking he could print his way out of debt. This thinking was similar as spending your way out of debt. Barry ordered the treasury to increase production! He must have mo money! By the end of his presidency, it cost more to print a hundred dollar bill than it was worth. As with most past government programs, sanity was never a factor. How does that work for you, Mr. Obama? This created hyper super doper inflation, where prices of goods increased daily. If you had paper money, it could not be saved, because later it had less value. If a loaf of bread could be found, the price soon reached $75. The value of US currency was backed by the full faith and credit of the Federal Government. The Federal Government was out of credit and everyone except the progressives lost faith. It is written on the front of a dollar bill" This Note is Legal Tender for all debts, Public and Private". It turned out that these were only "words"

Russia knew this day had to come. They had patiently waited for many years for America to destroy itself. Our major creditor, China panicked and sold its reserve of dollars. The premier of China, Hung Low Me Sag, flew into a rage when the last dollars China held, were now worthless. The Chinese Premier wondered how the one trillion dollars loaned to America would ever be re-paid. China's loans to America were held without collateral. Obama thought he could pass off worthless "paper" to settle the debt owed to other countries. He could financially screw the domestic bondholders of Federal Debt as with the bondholders during the Chrysler and Government Motors (GM) Union Bailout. If the domestic bondholders of American debt would not settle for pennies on the dollar, they were called greedy and selfish. The debt owed to other countries would be another matter.

Obama flew to Singapore to present his loan repayment scheme to the Chinese Premier. When Obama entered the meeting room of the Chinese Presidential Palace, he bent his body over like a pretzel, and while in the bent position, gave a wet kiss on the Premiers right hand. Obama said that it was an honor to be in the presence of the Supreme Communist Chinese Ruler. The Premier in disgust, made wild gestures and wiped his wet hand on Obama's sleeve. Once Obama returned to the upright position, he said he came bearing gifts. He had ten C-130 Hercules Aircraft packed with freshly printed one hundred dollar bills. This Obama reasoned is more than enough to repay China for the entire principal and Interest. Upon hearing the words of the "One", the Chinese Premier Hung Low Me Sag, flew into a mighty rage, saying in broken Chinese "Me Chinese, Not Stupid". He dismissed Obama like a servant, and said never to return without something of true value. President Obama, now totally dejected, made his last trip ever on Air Force One. To save precious fuel on the return trip to America, the ten C-130 Hercules dumped the now worthless currency at night over the Pacific Ocean. It was a beautiful sight to see millions of crisp freshly printed hundred dollar bills, gently floating in the cloudless sky, illuminated by the light of a full moon. It was a solemn day also for the Chinese. They wondered how the debt would be repaid, and who would buy their cheaply made products once sold in America. The Chinese Premier pondered the fate of China and how to recoup the bad loans made to America.

What would China repossess to recover the massive financial loss? American currency was worthless and the dept apparently unrecoverable. Had President Obama also squandered the American gold reserves? The Chinese Premier would take either Hawaii or Alaska in lieu of the defaulted American debt. We tried in vain to offer California in lieu of repaying the loan. Without entitlements most of the residents of California had already gone home to Mexico. An advantage of taking California is that many residents are already brainwashed. Why else would anyone vote for Nancy Pelosi? The Chinese Premier sternly replied to this offer "we might be communist, don't want that problem". "Don't have enough internment camps". "That place is full of nuts and berries". The younger Chinese Leaders set their sights on colonizing the Hawaiian Islands. Hawaii, beautiful group of lush tropical islands, would be a great Chinese vacation spot. The Chinese military longed dreamed of taking the military bases in Hawaii. These vital strategic locations would greatly aid the Chinese dream of world domination.

An added benefit is that the original inhabits of Hawaii were probably Chinese anyhow. The young beautiful Hawaiian Women can shake it better in those grass hula skirts than any Chinese. This idea caused problems at home with the straight Chinese Woman. The thought of the well endowed curvy Hawaiian Chinese American women mixing with their men caused ethnic Chinese women to be jealous and envy their Hawaiian counterparts. They told their men if they get "Lei" in Hawaii, they would never get "Lei" home in China.

The older wiser Chinese leaders, led by the Premier, knew that Hawaii, however beautiful, had few natural resources. Their eyes and thoughts of women had dimmed with age. They were concerned more with practical matters. Hawaii was strategically located and had several excellent harbors.

China now replaced America as a world superpower. It needed vast supplies of raw materials to fuel economic growth and continues its plans for world domination. The United States of America was now a footnote in history. China then filed suit in the world court to recoup their money loaned to America. No one was shocked with the unanimous verdict of the World Court. The international judges were blatantly anti-American. A French Judge on the world court stated after the verdict "The once arrogant mighty has fallen". Even the American Progressive Judge on the court voted in favor of the Chinese.

The Chinese Government after approval from the United Nations and with the legal verdict of the World Court foreclosed on all United States Federal Property in Alaska. To attempt to appease the people of Alaska, the Chinese Premier stated that the Chinese Government would not infringe upon current property rights of the State of Alaska and citizens. The State and citizens owned twenty eight percent of the land in Alaska. The Chinese knew that the people of Alaska were self reliant, independent and well armed. From watching the only channel on Chinese TV (Chi-Com 1), they were aware of the beauty of Alaska and that of its most famous citizen, Sara Palin. They also learned of her wisdom and that she was a straight shooter, in many ways. It is advisable for a communist or progressive, not to rile Sara or Todd Palin. (My favorite Palin has always been Piper)

The People's Republic of China now owned all land of the former United States of America in Alaska. Obama greatly protested the Chinese Alaskan Land Grab. He threatened sanctions against China with the United Nations, but China and Russia ignored his feeble pleas. Obama finally realized that for all his efforts of apologizing for America being an arrogant and evil country was for nothing. He engaged in his normal diplomacy, bend over, blame America for all the world's problems and talk, talk and talk. His final excuse is that he inherited the problem from George W., for he could do no wrong! Obama thought he was ordained by Allah to force his will upon man. He had special religious guidance from the radical mullahs and trained to deceive the masses. His words were sacrament, to be believed by the underclass without question.

When the Chinese Red Army entered Alaska, Obama ordered the military to stand down. Our military now completely demoralized and lacking funding and supplies had no choice but to retreat to the lower 48 states. The Chinese were nice enough to give our former fuel to our military so they could be transported to the lower 48 states. Without firing a shot, the Chinese at long last put the "American Dog in its Place". Michelle Obama stated: "that for the second time in her adult life, she was proud of America".

Alaska is a land of breathtaking natural beauty with vast untapped natural resources of timber, seafood, coal, gold, silver and oil and gas reserves. America was the first country in the history of the world to destroy its economy, lacking fiscal sanity, and leaving untouched unimaginable natural wealth. This ineptitude policy was at the behest of the environmentalist and progressives.

The American default of the trillion-dollar loan from China, led to a deal of the century for the Chinese. They now owned 270 million acres formerly part of the United States of America. Chinese plundered their resources of Alaska without regard to the environment. The plight of the polar bear, caribou or environmentalist would never hinder their exploitation. The vital offshore fishing areas of the North Sea and Bering Straits soon become sushi for the Chinese Fishing Industries. They had no concerns for a limited fishing season, size limits or any environmental concern. The once mighty Alaska fishing fleet, with no rights to the former federal waters, became nothing but a rusting ship graveyard. This symbolized the decline of a once great nation. Some ship captains ventured into waters now claimed by the Chinese. Alaskan ships were fired upon by the Chinese Navy, had their ships boarded and confiscated. The captured crews were led away in chains, many never to be seen again.

The people of Alaska were the most self sufficient and independent of all former Americans. Months after the Chinese occupied Alaska, the former American residents started to revolt against their cruel master. The Chinese response was to crush the bodies of the rioters without mercy. They cared not for the opinion of others in the world. The remnant of GE hoped to trade with China, so NBC and CNBC were instructed to have biased reporting towards the Chinese as they had the Progressives in the past. Many natives began to starve, with only limited access to hunting and fishing grounds and no means of employment. This started a southward migration of Alaskan's searching for hope.

The Red Army for target practice blasted American Bald Eagles out of the sky; until they were informed they were now Chinese Bald Eagles. Native Indian Totem Poles in Alaska were topped with a "Red Star". The people in China developed a taste for Caribou. Caribou by the tens of thousands were shot, butchered and their carcasses shipped back to the Chinese Mainland in massive refrigerated ships. The Caribou would never again peacefully graze near the warmth of the Alaskan oil pipeline. Timing was excellent since the Chinese had tired of dishes like "fish lips with celery" and "fish smell like pork".

Chinese had no concept of a wildlife "refuge". Baby seals were beat with chopsticks. They shot for sport animals native's needed for subsistence. This parallels the wasteful killing of the American Bison in the late 1800's by European American Hunters. This bison genocide, not for food or hide, was to starve the American Indian's into submission. History seems to always repeat itself!

The radical environmental groups were devastated by the Chinese raping of Mother Earth in Alaska. Greenpeace sent boats to the now Chinese waters of Alaska to stop whaling and killing of seals. The Chinese showing no mercy rammed and harpooned the Greenpeace boats, sending the boats and their crews to the bottom of the frigid Bering Sea. Further defeat for the environmentalist was watching the diesel fuel rise to the waters surface, from their sunken wrecks. This formed a massive oil slick soiling local beaches and sea creatures, both large and small. Members of the Red Army instead of cleaning the diesel soaked sea birds, set them on fire. After finish cooking the birds they sat around a fire eating "Peking Duck". The Chinese love to gamble on any event. They wagered on how far a bird on fire can fly. Captured "Greenies" were forced the watch the birds ablaze as part of their punishment.

The "Greenies" then climbed trees to stop the Chinese Loggers. This approach always worked when protesting in America, especially in California. The loggers were paid a bonus for cutting down these trees. Enjoying the moment, the Chinese loggers did not offer the traditional "Tim ber", [mu cai] in Chinese. Without warning the tree with the attached greenie fell with a great crash. This was a great way to tenderize an environmentalist. After a few "thumping's" Greenies environmental zeal quickly began to wane. Greenies then laid their bodies on logging roads to protest logging. Being on the ground must give better results than protesting in a tree. Who knew that Chinese dozers and logging trucks lacked brakes? Environmentalist for some reason soon lost their radical zeal for protesting trying to save mother earth. There was little learning in a Chinese re-education camp. Their numbers painfully dwindled and the Chinese prevented the remnant of the old line media from documenting their loss. Did an environmentalist fall if no one could see or hear their demise!

Their Druid Style Religion had contributed to the downfall of the country. This economic destruction was directly tied to out of control government spending and denying U.S. access to our natural resources. Did the greenies care if gasoline was $7.0 a gallon or the unemployment rate was 25 per cent? When your religion is a tree, you weep at its falling. When nature is killing nature, greenie weenies were totally impotent. Their motto "nature destroying nature is good but man is always bad".

The conservationist in the past, had a deep love of nature, and tried to balance the needs of society, while preserving nature. I respect my trees, especially the beautiful Japanese maple costing $250. The beauty of the tree and the joy it gives is priceless. That tree's wish is my command. I will give it a hug and even sing a tune to keep it happy. I live in a beautiful place in harmony with nature. Sometimes nature sucks, like when the carpenter ants kill my hundred year plus mature mighty oaks. I must use an evil pesticide to keep nature from destroying itself. Killing the ant invaders to save a majestic tree is a good compromise.

The greenies did their part to destroy the economy and therefore the country. When conservation was high jacked by the radical environmental movement, the environmental cause became another means to redistribute wealth and to gain control over the population. Progressives must use lies and propaganda to advance their cause. Why else if the people were not deceived, would anyone in their right mind follow their lead? This was the golden path of progressive enlightenment, paved with good intentions using the wealth of others. The environmental movement became another tentacle of the progressive movement. In the 1970's there was the alarm of global cooling. We were all going to freeze to death! Twenty years later we were all going to die due to global warming. They were constantly sounding the environmental alarms. The term "Climate Change" was coined so an Environmentalist could never be proven wrong. Any change in climate proved their theory and it was all the fault of man!

Middle Tennessee had major flooding from torrential rainfall the first of May 2010. Many streams are clogged with debris. The stream and river channels need to be straightened, widened and have the debris removed. This would afford better drainage and reduce the potential for flood damage. What hinders or stops flood prevention measures? Answer: Greenie Weenies and the Progressive lackeys in Government.

In California environmental regulations inhibit the removal of dead brush from the hillsides. This would limit damage from a wildfire. When there is a fire with all the accumulated fuel, all creatures large and small perish. Before Environmentalist, nature had numerous small fires in the forest that removed the dead trees, limbs and leaf litter. These frequent smaller fires being less intense would not damage the existing trees and actually promoted new growth and recycled nutrients to the soil.

Many years ago the alarm was what is killing the frogs. Greenie's thought the demise of the frogs was an early indicator of environmental damage.

We must make radical changes to our standard of living and way of life! What did happen to the frogs? They are all hopping in my yard. By all accounts of their vast numbers, the frogs are doing all right. If you need a few thousand frogs, I will be glad to sell all you can croak.

I'm glad the environmentalist never learned of my five legged frogs. They have two legs in front and three legs in the rear. The frogs became confused whether to leap or pole vault. If the greenies heard about this, they would file a lawsuit with a greenie judge. The verdict would be that I could never mow or even walk on my grass. Where could my dogs go to relieve themselves? My new home would have to be demolished, removing all vestiges of man. Is that not the dream of every radical environmentalist!

The State of North Carolina v. Tennessee Valley Authority

This lawsuit alleges pollution primarily from Tennessee and the Tennessee Valley Authority is damaging the environmental health in North Carolina. Months back while visiting the Great Smokey National Park in Tennessee and North Carolina I noticed many trees that were dead or dying. As a lover of nature, this was quite distressing. Maybe this was why North Carolina had filed the lawsuit?

"This case, if unchallenged and overturned, could embolden environmental activists and left-wing judges to begin to create piecemeal environmental regulations on all kinds of socially and economically beneficial conduct and thus usurp the proper function of the political branches of the government," warns Brian Walsh, senior legal research fellow at the Heritage Foundation.

"The other worst-case scenario," Walsh adds, "is that politically minded governors and attorneys general in some states can force neighboring states through the federal courts to engage in odious environmental exercises and make themselves look good with no political cost to themselves."

"You can't prove where the pollution is coming from, The Tennessee Valley Authority says, and North Carolina has sources in its State", said Maureen Martin, senior fellow for legal affairs at the Heartland Institute. "Nothing would prevent South Carolina from suing North Carolina by saying that the pollution is being sent their way. Or England could say that we're blowing air pollution over to them. North Carolina winning this case could potentially cause that kind of insanity."

Thank you Mr. North Carolina attorney general for raising my electric bill. The only people who benefit from this madness are the politicians of North Carolina, lawyers and wacko environmental groups. When I first heard about air pollution from the Tennessee Valley Authority killing trees in the Great Smokey Mountains, I wondered what the truth was. Shortly after I poised this question, I was enlightened.

The following is from the National Park Service, US Department of the Interior:" Eastern hemlock trees are some of the largest and most common trees in the Great Smoky Mountains. Unfortunately, they are under attack from a non-native insect called the hemlock wooly adelgid. Without successful intervention, the hemlock woolly adelgid is likely to kill most of the hemlock trees in the parks.

Called the "redwood of the east," eastern hemlocks (Tsuga canadenis) can grow more than 150 feet tall on trunks measuring six feet in diameter. Some hemlocks in the park are over 500 years old.

Over 800 acres of old-growth hemlocks trees grow in the Smokies-more than in any other national park. Younger hemlock forests cover an additional 90,000 acres of land in the park. Originally discovered here in 2002, adelgid infestations have now spread throughout the park's hemlock forests. In some areas infested trees have already begun to die. "

A question of the above statement is "What intervention". Intervention would mean spraying the hemlock wooly adelgid with an evil pesticide. A greenie weenie would have an environmental panic attack and file a lawsuit to save the pest. If these beautiful hemlock trees were on my property, it would be all out war on the Adelgid. I would like to spit some beechnut in that bugs eye. Progressives and Environmentalist often must resort to lies, half-lies and distorting facts and data to further their agenda. To the attorney general of North Carolina; I want my damn money back! This is not the behavior expected of a Near Southern Gentleman or Woman.

If the radical environment groups had believed in the one true God, the outcome would be quite different. My Savior, not the Groper in Chief, Al Gore, will never disappoint in life or in death. I live in a beautiful place, surrounded by the Godly made wonders of nature. It cannot compare to the place prepared for me in paradise. We will be forced to bear heavy burdens. God will lighten the load of all who believe.

I am a conservationist. All that is needed to improve my ecological progress is money. The dead and dying oaks need to be removed, both standing and fallen. Please send a tree surgeon to save my trees. Translation - More Wealth = Greater Conservation. If I were very wealthy, I would have four acres of my property covered with the finest fescue sod. The local deer population would never leave my gourmet greenery. My yard would be the envy of all the neighbors. The throngs of frogs would be pleased.

Cutting your grass in the future will be viewed by some as decadence since there will be a great shortage of gasoline. With a large stockpile fuel and no job or place to go, why not have a well-manicured yard? It would be worth all the expense and effort to see the expression of any passing environmentalist on foot or bicycle. Their faces would display such bitterness; it would remind me of Helen Thomas. Thank God my house is 350' from the road. When it comes to my carbon footprint, as it has often been said, bigger is better.

Thousands of high wage union job in Alaska tied to the fishing, timber, minerals and oil and gas industry were now lost. Anwr became a Chinese full service gas station. There were no trees to hug there anyhow! According to the Sarah Palin, Alaska accounted for nearly 20 % of U.S. Oil and Gas production. An analysis by the University of Alaska Anchorage showed the oil industry supported as many as 110,000 jobs in Alaska (one-third of the state's workforce), including funding for three-quarters of state government jobs. The Chinese non-union workers were thrilled to take the American Jobs. This completed an American Job replacement program that was started by the Chinese years earlier. With the loss of Alaska, the former United States lost its oil and gas reserves, valuable mineral deposits along with prime fishing grounds. The Chinese had everything needed to be the sole superpower in the world.

After it was too late, the progressives and environmentalist in the former USA realized that if their former country had these resources, it would have been used in a more eco-friendly manner and the proceeds would ease or eliminate the depression that gripped the country. They finally learned that the capitalism system benefited the consumer, workers, employers, government and environment. The currency of the USA was nearly worthless. When we owned the resources of Alaska, we had something of value to barter. As the economy declined, so did the environment.

Many conservatives voiced the prediction of economic doom for many years if America did not drastically reduce government spending and the massive budget deficits. President George W. Bush did his part to move America to an economic tipping point, spending without control and a lax casual attitude towards illegal immigration. The only good about a moderate Republican, is that are not as bad as a progressive. President Obama in his effort to remake an "unjust Country" accelerated the largest annual deficit spending of his predecessor by 4 times to 1.9 trillion for the fiscal budget year of 2010. Most of the reckless spending from the stimulus plan, auto union and Wall Street bailouts were poorly planned and executed. The auto union in the GM and Chrysler bailouts got the goldmine and we got the shaft. The majority of the politicians, who voted for these bills, never read, understood or cared of which they voted. They only voted to appease Pelosi, Reed and "The One". By yielding their political power, they were good little progressives. The growing opposition of the American People to the out of control federal spending came too late and would not deter Obama's reckless spending. Towards the end he was forced to reduce spending. He desperately needed bailout loans from the World Bank. These loans came with restrictive financial strings. The World Bank dictated financial policy for the country. All spending by the federal government must be cut by 25% across the board and taxes increased. This also included the salaries and benefits of all government workers, those on Social Security and all entitlement programs. The government employee union bosses called for a strike. Other union organizers sent their members out to protest. The Takers started to riot. They said: "We worked for our money, you ain't taking it away". Rioters overturned vehicles, broke store windows and went of a "shopping spree". Murder and mayhem spread throughout the cities.

Barack presence and word was now on television and radio 24/7. He said: You have nothing to Fear, for I am the "One". "Look into my eyes, hear my words, all who come to me will be comforted". God hearing his words thought of sending lightening bolts to shock him into sanity. Upon further contemplation, God said Obama was not worth the effort. If Obama was a computer program, he would be an unrecoverable error for the American People.

Note to Obamanites: The party is over! The fighting in the streets worsened. The shedding of blood, death, and the cries of the afflicted was everywhere. The police first used water cannons without success on the rioters. The riots grew in intensity. Embattled police were forced to use tear gas, rubber bullets and soon fearing for their lives, real bullets. Many police and rioters were injured or worst. The rioters were beyond control. The rioters seemed not to fear death. Maybe it was the influence of drugs, alcohol or the mob mentality. Those who mistakenly believed in Black Liberation Theology were leaders of the riots. They could multi-task being a community agitator while still searching for the "Promised Land".
It was too dangerous for the news media to record the events. Upon hearing of the departure of the media, Jesse Jackson and AL Sharpton were forced to leave the field of action. Why agitate when you can't be on television, radio or profit from blackmail. After much destruction and loss of life, the riots were temporally quelled.

Barrack lusted for social justice through redistribution of the wealth to the "rightful owners." Whatever the cost to society, he would get even! He knew that reparations alone, would never be sufficient to punish the evil European - Americans, and fully atone for their past racial intolerance. In a mad panic Barrack was attempting to empty the treasury. He knew his time was running out.

The name of my God was never invoked except when they used his name in vain or when the "Takers" demanded "Christian Charity". This was just another lame excuse why they were due the fruits of the labor of others. If the Takers studied the word of God, they would know they would not qualify or deserve "Christian Charity".

Expect Christian Charity

Expect Christian Charity, to live a heathen life
Provide their every need, please punish me
Work every day, they watch Oprah
Didn't cause the recession, suffer anyway
No work, no credit' Barney don't care
A home loan for everyone: goodbye economy
Unwed mothers, no morals, no worries
They bore the problems, we pay the price
Sperm Donors abound, then nowhere to be found
They have the pleasure, I have the grief
Country near bankrupt, I pay my bills
Many live for today, taxpayer's handle tomorrow

Ancient Prophesy

There once existed in Central America a highly advanced Mayan Culture. They were noted for the only fully developed written language of Pre-Columbian America. They excelled at art, architecture, mathematics and astronomy. The Maya Calendar was very sophisticated and extremely accurate. Their Calendar predicted the end of the world in the year of my lord, 2012. Did the Mayan's know of the coming of Barack Husein Obama? How could they know that a charismatic historic transformative man lacking wisdom would arise? Those Mayan intellectuals must have been aliens. How could any man accurately predict that future? The prophecy was so grim, that in panic they fled from their cities hundreds of years before his coming.

Most prophecy is very vague, so anything they have said or written could be construed as true. These prophets are often deceased for hundreds of years before their predications become realized. We are soon to witness the wisdom of the Mayans, expressed many years ago.

Atop the Mayan temple many important procedures were undertaken. Mayan Priests performed the first open heart surgery. Using a flint knife, they cut open the chest of those sacrificed and held up the still beating heart to the delight of the crowd. Then the sacrificed moved on to the next stage.

The Mayan created many inventions still used today. Most notably was the early form of the "Chop a matic". With just one swipe of your hand, the head of those sacrificed would be cleanly cut. I was sold on the product after the first demonstration shown on the Mayan Home Shopping Network. The Mayan Priest and gathered crowd watched with delight as the severed head bounced down the steps of the temple. Children learned math by counting the number of bounces made by the severed sacrificial heads. In unison they counted out loud - 1, 2, 3, 4, - - - - - - - - - -. A new show was started called "As the head bounces". It was the number one educational program on Mayan Public Theatre. (MPT)

How could the Mayan's predict our doom but not their own? A recent discovery at a Mayan Temple yielded information on the end of their culture around 900 AD.

The following words were the last ever carved in Stone by the Mayan's: "Liberals took over; many people stopped working, depended on government" the final words were "king emptied treasury, and went broke". The Liberals in Mayan Government at first was pleased with this early form of "Social Justice". It guaranteed forever they thought the support of the people. They created the original "Takers". The remaining producers were taxed and regulated until they could no longer carry the financial and moral burdens of society. The Mayan King had emptied the treasury to appease the takers and the civilization collapsed. The ancient Takers then rioted, demanding social justice. The riot turned violent, with the Takers robbing, killing, raping and doing all kinds of insidious activities. Once stolen supplies were depleted, with no producers left to support them, the people of the Taker Tribe had no choice but to abandon the cities and blend into the countryside, forever searching for someone to blame.

The Mayan culture disappeared well before the arrival of the Spanish Europeans. Unlike many ethnic groups, they had no other racial groups to blame for their shortcomings.

I greatly admired the Native American culture. With limited means to exploit their environment they lived in closer harmony with nature than their European counterparts. Their original domain extended over North, South America and the Islands of the Caribbean, including Jamaica and Haiti. They had a long and beautiful culture, which was destroyed by illegal immigration. The original native populations displaced by illegal immigrants died by disease, starvation or violence. This was the result of mans early failure to control its borders. Below are the comments of a great Native American about this subject:

Before our white brothers arrived to make us civilized men, we didn't have any kind of prison. Because of this, we had no delinquents. Without a prison, there can be no delinquents. We had no locks nor keys and therefore among us there no thieves. When someone was so poor that he couldn't afford a horse, a tent or a blanket, he would, in that case, receive it all as a gift. We were too uncivilized to give great importance to private property. We didn't know any kind of money and consequently, the value of a human being was not determined by his wealth. We had no written laws laid down, no lawyer, and no politicians, therefore we were not able to cheat and swindle one another. We were really in bad shape before the white men arrived and I don't know how to explain how we were able to manage without these fundamental things that (so they tell us) are so necessary for a civilized society.
John (Fire) Lame Deer Sioux Lakota - 1903-1976

A nation without borders is not a nation - Ronald Reagan. History has a funny way of repeating itself, or what goes around is here! A nation that is political correct (PC) will not defend its borders or make any hard choices pertaining to their wards. This kindness will allow a parasite to devour the organism from the inside out. The country is just a shell of its former self. This is the outcome of people who hold no absolute truths. Is this not another version of Montezuma's revenge?

Modern Prophesy

You cannot save the country, for it is beyond repair. Make sure you are prepared so you family can survive the days to come.

It was foretold long ago that a great sage would arise at a time of doom. The time is now, the man is Glenn Beck.

GLENN BECK "ORACALE OF DOOM"

Those brave Americans, who watched and listened to Glen Beck, knew the beginning of the end commenced in early 2009. Glenn arose as an ancient prophet preaching to the masses in the political and economic wasteland. Many heard his cries for action, only a few took him as serious. Many on the left tried to discredit and silence him. Day after day, Glen tirelessly pleaded for the leaders of the country to repent, change from their evil ways and be fiscally responsible. Glen created charts, graphs, drew chalkboard illustrations and gave speeches till his voice cracked. Towards the end, he even resorted to hand puppets to get his point across. Often he would be brought to tears, the unbridled raw emotion and his love of God, family and country. I often worried that Glen went near the edge of insanity, but thankfully, at the last instance, normalcy would always return. His wife and family always had a calming effect. Tania, his beloved wife however petite, could always keep Glen under control. To Tania-Your country owes you more in gratitude than we can ever express!

Many of the companies that advertised on the Glen Beck radio and television shows offered a plan to survive an economic downturn. There was Goldline (1-866-Gold-line) who pleaded day after day that you must have gold as part of your investment portfolio. Their experts predicted gold could reach $2000 an ounce by 2011. Glen himself bought gold by the shovel load, not as an investment, but as a security plan for his family.

The only difference between toilet paper and paper currency is that government says one is legal tender. Its supposed value is based upon the full faith and credit of the United States. What if there is no faith in the government and its credit meant nothing? It will come to pass that a hundred dollar bill and toilet paper will have the same value, to wipe your butt! The toilet paper might be a better choice of the two, particularly if it is the six ply Charmin Creamy Deluxe Brand. At least the toilet paper would be sanitary. I heard the words of Glen Beck and commercials from Goldline but lack funds to buy silver or gold. I called Goldline and was interested in purchasing twenty million dollars worth of gold. This was only an academic exercise, since I had no money.

This reminds me of an 80-year-old man, withered in every way, sitting on a park bench on a lovely spring day. In front of his eyes walks by a beautiful scanty clad young well-endowed woman. Her silky wind blown hair and the graceful movements of her body was like poetry in motion. The old man knew he could do nothing but sit there and drivel. He tried to whistle as in the days of old. The sound that exited his parched lips was that only the dogs in the park could hear, and they began to bark in reply. The old man, now devastated, could only imagine what his faint whistle meant to the dogs, and trembled at the meaning of their answer. Mr. Beck, I hear you but cannot obey. The mind is willing but the wallet is empty. Your words ring true, but like the old man I cannot respond.

Another of Glen Beck's advertisers is selling nutritious yummy survival food. Glen says he has a year's supply of survival food. . The products are probably freeze dried or canned. I think the products would be like freeze dried beef stroganoff, or some likely proximity. I would suggest storing hundreds of pounds of rice (if you are in a hurry, buy the minute kind); Betty Crocker scalloped dried potatoes (yum) by the case, tons of powered milk, coffee, water by the gallon and any other products with a long shelf life. Toilet paper could be stored forever if it doesn't get wet. Recently in the socialist utopia of Cuba, toilet paper was rationed. Since Fidel completely controls the Cuban population, they get only the cheap rough half ply variety, when it is in season. In a pinch, it serves well as sand paper. You know that Fidel and his henchmen at the top of the political food chain have only the best of cigars, women, and food and of course, Charmin Extra Creamy 6 ply toilet paper. The correct name of the paper actually used by the Cuban Peasants is tree hugger supreme. This trait is held in common with Fidel's radical environmental terrorist friends.

I am an overweight European-American. Fat people like myself, can survive much longer without food than skinny people. To all the slim, well built individuals who ever made fun of fat people, I will feel terrible watching you wither, suffer and pass. God has provided me with a built-in food pantry. I would survive without food for a month or two, as long as I have gallons of bottle water. It would be my luck; I would be like the fat guy on "LOST." He lived on a deserted island, struggling to survive, but never losing an ounce. Life is not fair! Necessities in my survival food supplies would be a year's supply of Hershey's 60% dark chocolate bars in the 3.52-ounce size. This delightful treasure of complex flavors consumed with a cold glass of Carnation Brand Powered milk, would make the worldly problems temporarily fade away.

NOTE TO GLENN BECK: Everyone knows you have gold enough to "shovel "and a years supply of yummy survival food. With difficult times around the corner, "what are you goanna do when the takers come for you"? Unlike other wealthy people who have assets in real estate, stock market and banks, Glen has provided lasting security for his family by buying gold. I am sure any security guard in the future working for Glen will gladly take a 1920 AU Double Eagle Gold Coin in compensation for a weeks work. To you other wealthy individuals that waited too late to buy gold _ GOODBYE

Another Glen Beck Show advertiser is selling non-hybrid seeds enough to grow a one-acre survival garden. Growing your own vegetables is an excellent way to provide your family with fresh nutritious food. Along with a good variety of seeds, you need fertilizer and a tiller or some other device to prepare the soil for planting. To operate the tiller, you must have a reservoir of the evil carbon producing gasoline. You should be carbon neutral since the plants will adsorb the deadly greenhouse gas Co2 that the gasoline operated tiller and your bodily functions emit.

Start now preparing your soil for gardening. If the soil is acidic, add lime. I think my garden patch needs a truckload of sand. Sand is a very important additive if the soil has high clay content. Spread evenly the plant growth enhancers over the garden. In the fall, plow or till all the above ingredients plus manure into the soil. You don't want all the crap in one area. Bull Crap is readily available from the old mainline press. Leftist newspapers and magazines should not be read, just shredded and mixed into your garden. What came from the ground should be returned to Mother Earth. In early spring, till and further prepare the soil for the insertion of seeds or baby plants after the dreaded tax day of April 15th. Remember your produce is one asset the government has not learned how to confiscate or tax.

I must admit farming is not in my DNA. My earthly father in Heaven is laughing at my exploits in farming. Many years ago, my father asked me to plow a field on his farm. Dad left me there alone while he ran an errand. After some time a relative came by and said I was plowing the wrong direction. I thought Dad had one on those multi-directional plows. My Dad was proud of that John Deere Tractor he thought was made in America. I sure hated to tell him that a sticker of the tractor said "Made in England". Dad still loved that tractor, but his American Pride was slightly diminished. When it comes to farming, the effort is there, but knowledge is lacking. My corn plants grow fine if you like the midget variety.

We could grow corn like the ancient Native American Indians; dig a hole, deposit seeds and preferably a dead fish for fertilizer. Your garden would need only Sunshine, the poisonous gas CO_2 (according to AL Gore) and water. Even today Mexican Farmer's fertilize their crops at the beginning and end of each row. These vegetables are always the juiciest.

To preserve your vegetables, you must learn how to can. Actually it should be called "Jarring", since you use a glass jar. Listed below are some tips:

* Choose fresh produce picked at the moment of perfection
* Use glass jars so you can see the type and condition of your food
* Wash all produce

* drop the produce gently in the jar
* Set up jar cooker with racks
* Heat the jar to the prescribed temperature and proper time of cooking
* Slap on a lid and let the jar cool

Equipment you will need:
Pressure cooking with a temperature gauge
* Pressure cooker racks to keep the jars from banging
* Tongs or your wife has quick reflexes to lift the jars out of boiling water
* Oven mitts to handle hot jars
* Glass jars, lids and band aides

The above information was lifted from "Cooking: Basics of canning your own fruits and vegetables." Being a male chauvinist, I will leave this chore to my wife.

Refrigeration was once used to preserve perishable food, but now worthless without electricity. The Takers can never learn the canning procedures, since it requires effort. Our Aunt Sherry's canned green beans sure are tasty on a cold winter's night. Tennessee County hams, salted and cured to perfection, would last forever without refrigeration.
The most important product or service not advertised on Glen's Radio show is guns and ammo. This essential life and property saving device should be the first on any Conservatives (Producers) Shopping List.

1. Short barrel 12 Gauge Pump Shotgun. Excellent arm and shoulder exercise while you pump and fire. This is the most effective weapon for close range combat. Don't worry about accuracy, just point and shoot. It works equally well with the Obama Civil Defense Force "OCDF" or the "Takers". To keep your attackers attention, alternate ammunition for your shotgun with 00 Buckshot, rifled slugs and birdshot. Using a variety of ammunition ensures your attackers will never get bored. Remember, variety is the spice of life.
2. Smith and Wesson 9 mm M&P semi automatic Pistol. You must carry a least 10 magazines, loaded with nothing less than the finest hollow point ammo money can buy. To double the effect buy two pistols, one for each hand. This will require special training to enhance hand eye coordination. It looks cool on Television when a good guy is shooting with two pistols

and the empty magazines fall to the ground, reloads and keep on firing. I also like the laser pointers piercing light especially in a darken room. Warning: Use of laser pointers could give up your location. Never point the laser light into the eyes of your attacker. If the attacker survives your hollow points, he might sue you for retinal damage. Boo Hoo! I can already imagine the lawyers advertising - "If you sustained retinal damage from a laser sight, and survived the hollow points, please contact B.O.'s Law firm in Chicago at 999-424-6666. We have extorted millions of dollars for our clients."

3. 30-30 semiautomatic rifle with 10 loaded magazines, each containing 50 rounds. A high power quality scope is essential, since this weapon is used for long distance targets. It is always best to never let your opposition get close. I guarantee they will look and smell better at a distance.

A minimum of a thousand rounds of ammo is required for each weapon. You never want to run out of ammo in the middle of the action. Enjoy the moment, for you are now a defender of liberty. In summary, a 30-30 rifle for ranges out to 250', 9 MM semiautomatic pistol for intermediate distance and most important is the 12-gauge shotgun when it gets up close and personal.

I have signs in my yard to mark the proper firing distance and to denote the type of weapon and ammunition to be used. This would assure that any criminal with evil intent trespassing on my property knows exactly what to expect. These posted signs are legal notification per advice from my attorney. My range markers are shown below:

I was puzzled when the box of my Winchester 243 Win CXP-2 Ammunition has a warning label stating: "Use for light, thin skinned game". This prompted immediate action to upgrade to a Winchester 30-30 Rifle.

Stock up now while you can, the Perky Progressives cannot tolerate a well-armed, self-sufficient population. They will use the EPA to regulate out of existence lead used in bullets. If I am forced to shoot someone, I would hate to think they might get lead poisoning. What they cannot legislate, they will regulate. If "Cap and Trade" legislation will not pass, let the EPA declare harmless $Co2$ a toxic substance. By regulation or executive order, the will of Obama will be done! The wishes of the people be damned! He after all is Lord Obama.

The Red Government's plan is to place taxes on guns and ammo of up to 500%. This will greatly reduce production and sales of guns and ammo. Obama will sell this plan as raising needed taxes, to reduce budget deficits he has created. If this idea falls short, the old standby to justify raising taxes is "It's for the Children". The "Great One" proclaimed often during the presidential campaign in 2008, "that if you make less than 250K a year, you will not pay one extra penny in taxes". I would guarantee that most of the gun owners make fewer than 250 K.

Secondly all gun owners must be registered with the "OCDF, (Obama Civilian Defense Force)." Tracking devices will be built into every new weapon sold in America. Your government will know where you are at all times, even if you don't. Your ammo will be personally engraved at the time of purchase with the owner's information. This act will limit the number of outlets allowed to sell ammo and double the price of the product. If your ammo is ever stolen and used in the commission of a crime, the registered owner will be 'in a world of hurt".

A Progressive or Communist Government cannot permit an armed population. They will first ask nicely for you to turn in your weapons, saying the action will reduce crime. Our Socialist friends in England successfully implemented this plan several years ago. After WW2, the British made a left turn. I think the English also attempted that same plan to confiscate weapons here in America back around 1776. How well did that program work out? After the failure of the voluntary weapon surrender, Obama strikes into action. The Thugs of the "OCDF", Moslem Brotherhood and "The New Black Panther Party" fresh with GPS coordinates of the address to your front door gathered by Obama's Census Worker's, sweep down in the middle of night, like a horde of Mongols, confiscating weapons and ammo. This night, know forever as "Up Yours", went terribly out of control. The Thugs not only stole guns and ammo, but food, gold, silver, diamonds, other personal property and liberty. I learned a valuable lesson from the gun instructor at Guns and Leather in Greenbrier, Tennessee. He said" that when the government comes for your weapons, give them the ammunition first". This proves that I did pay attention in the gun safety class. There were many nice ladies in this class. A pistol packing Mama is sexy thing. In this instance caliber does matter.

Another reason why you should never surrender your weapons is they are a vital piece of farming equipment. To keep the pesky critters away from your vegetable garden you need a 12 gauge pump short barrel shotgun loaded with 00 buckshot. This will be required when your vegetables are ripe for the picking. Unknown forces known as the "Takers" quietly sit in their easy chairs, watching closely your months of hard work. You might think they are the un-dead, since they have not moved in weeks. Actually they are saving their strength so they can steal you blind, when your produce is ready to harvest. If the Progressives still have political control, they might force the producers to pick their produce, prepare the food and feed it to the "Takers". I pray the Progressives with their unholy political power are soon vanquished.

The Takers are nocturnal creatures, sleeping late into the day. With electricity being a historical fact, their woman had nothing to do during the day. It was a good thing that for most Takers sexual activity did not require electricity or batteries. Never again could they watch "Oprah". Nearing sunset they start to carouse, and prepare for another night of theft, mayhem and pillage. Even in total darkness you sensed they were close. At some distance the smell of death and clangor of "Bling" gave away their location. They always attacked when the wind direction was to their favor.

Many "Taker" females might require extra penetration. This is due to all the hard fat, accumulated from years of excessive snacking sitting on their fat Asses watching "Oprah". The girth of some female "Taker" might be startling at first, but remember the bigger they are, the harder they fall. The females are slower of foot than the males. The first wave of attackers will be the "Taker" men, followed by the slower women. Morbidly Fat "Taker women charging towards you at full speed, is an unsettling sight. Their various body parts move completely at random with every step. If their gyrations of their body parts are synchronized, it could be an earth-shaking event. The sight of the advancing "taker" women might cause you to retreat or at a minimum to "lose your Lunch". At all cost of life or limb, you must hold your position. A key point to remember is that the "Taker" women tire quickly; there is no need to panic. There will be time to regain your composure and re-load.

WARNING - Watching the movie "Zombieland" does not make an expert on this matter. The one fact learned from the movie, is to always seal the deal with a double tap. This guarantees they will never rise again. It is hard to determine when a "Taker" is playing possum. By nature they are extremely sedentary.

If ammo runs short, let them move in closer and only fire when you see the "whites of their eyes". This old phrase is only used in context to determine proximity, and not a racial term. "Takers" (as with Zombies) are comprised of all races, sexes and of many national origins. When battling the "Takers", save the final round for you, if all hope are lost. Before taking this final action, hold us a sign that says "WORK". You must yell the word when holding this sign. Some Takers cannot read or did not have this word in their limited vocabulary. This will cause most of the Takers to panic and retreat. This is their most dreaded "four letter word", always to be avoided. Some Takers might temporarily stop their attack and ask you what that word means. I overheard a Taker women say that "Obama" said they would never have to do that!

A typical "Taker" conversation on October 8, 2009 with Ken Rogulski reporting on WJR in Michigan

Rogulski:	Why are you here?
Taker Female #1:	To get some money.
Rogulski:	What kind of money?
Taker Female # 1:	Obama money.
Rogulski:	Where's it coming from?
Taker Female:	Obama.
Rogulski:	And where did Obama get it?
Taker Female #1:	I don't know his stash. I don't know. (Laughter) I don't know where he got it from, but he givin' it to us, to help us.
Taker Female #2:	and we love him. That's why we voted for him!
Taker's:	(chanting) Obama! Obama! Obama! (laughing)

This unfortunately represented the views of the "Taker's" in the good ole days when every thing was given and nothing was expected except your vote for the Progressives.

A typical "Taker" conversation on October 8, 2012 with Ken Rogulski reporting on WJR in Michigan

Rogulski:	Why are you rioting?
Taker Female # 1:	No Damn welfare
Taker Female #2:	We worked for it!
Rogulski:	You worked for it?
Taker Female #2:	Yea, we supported Obama, the Democrats
Rogulski:	Why steal murder and destroy?
Taker Female #1:	They said, we didn't have to
Rogulski:	Have to what?
Taker Female #1	Work!
Rogulski	Where did the money come from?
Taker female #2:	I don't know, Obama's Stash
Takers:	(chanting) we earned it, we want it, we goanna get some.
Rogulski:	Help! Help! (Gurgle sound, inaudible, silence)

The "Takers"

My earliest memory of seeing a "Taker' was around 1979. This was about fifteen years into the Democratic Party vote conditioning and voter breeding program. I was a married poor graduate student at Memphis State University. Producers often make sacrifices and deny themselves income or possessions, for the hope of future monetary gains. An example would be a Doctor spending many years and thousands of dollars in Medical School, so one day their efforts will pay dividends. Another example is starting a small business. Often for the first year, you hope to break even after expenses. Dave Ramsey refers to this as "Delayed Pleasure". This is doing without material things today for the expectation of future gains. This relates to the old concept of "Pay me now or pay me later". This concept is something a Taker could never understand. They expect instant gratification and expect it free of charge.

My wife and I were shopping for groceries at Montessi's Supermarket in Memphis Tennessee. We had little money and bought the bare essentials. Nearing the checkout, there was a large woman in front of us. Her grocery basket was filled to the brim with hams, steaks, a giant frozen turkey and many other choice and delicious items. Once the cashier finished ringing up the woman's groceries, the woman pulled out a thick wad of food stamps and paid the cashier. I looked at my wife and my meager items of beans, bread and a small round steak, and just shook my head. There at the cash register at Montessi's Supermarket, I made a pledge that when I go to work after graduate school, I would eat as well as that woman on food stamps. From my appearance, you know that pledge was honored.

The multi-generational "Takers" who benefited from government largess and wealth transfer from the producers, were thrilled with Progressive Programs during the first three years of Obama's Regime. The "Takers" were conditioned and trained for over fifty years to support the Democratic Party. Behavior modification began at an early age. "Sesame Street" was instructed to place special emphasis on the letter "D". After all, the show was on public television. In practice voting sessions, if they voted correctly for Democrats, a government treat would be dispensed. Panic arose when election boards wanted to remove the party affiliations and just list the candidate's name. This caused such anxiety in the "Taker" community that the idea was quickly dropped. Introducing an additional factor requiring thought was too much stress. This reward based conditioning lasted for the entire life of a "Taker". Election Day became more important that Christmas. "Takers" would arise early, bathe and put on their finest clothes. This must be a special day, since the "Takers" never behaved in this manner. They waited anxiously for the government sponsored vans to arrive to take them to the polling center. Democrats on site would usher them to the voting machine and prayed to Karl Marx the years of training would not be forgotten. After voting, they were fed lunch and returned home. This process was the same, year after year for countless generations.

You might be poor if:

1. No daddy, just a sperm donor (You were not a test-tube baby)
2. All brothers and sisters are half brothers and sisters
3. Mother at age 15, grandmother by age 30 & great grandmother at age 45
4. Colt 45 is your favorite beer and handgun
5. Your Momma has a revolving man door to her bedroom.

The mindless loyalty of the "Takers" was firmly cemented by the "government bribes", years of conditioning and the glowing aura of "The One". He said" give me your blind allegiance and you will want for nothing". In him they completely followed, hanging on every word. It did not matter if his words were utter nonsense. He was after all, a historic figure! Who knew history could be so horrendous?

The Takers had neurotic lifestyle adjustments, after the downfall of the country. They never earned their way, thinking work was something only done by some unlucky people. "Takers" were products of a social justice experiment that went terribly wrong. The progressive social justice cabal had total control of the federal government with the coronation of President Obama, and controlling majorities in the Senate and House of Representatives. The embattled Conservatives, lacking political power, were delegated to the men's and little girls' room. Republicans were just a group of politicians the Progressives accused of hindering "Hope and Change". The Republicans held no real power; however Obama still called them the party of "No". Obama and his political followers of merry men and women would bring to fruition, No Money, No Country, No Hope. A glimmer of hope appeared whe Republicans gained control of Congress after the November 2, 2010 election. This positive "change" as the story of my life, was too little, too late. The country still had Obama as President and Harry Reid in charge of the Senate.

The "Great Society" had provided the Takers with cradle to the grave welfare for many generations. The Takers never learned values, work ethic or personal responsibility, believing forever that by voting for the Democrats, the social gravy train and "Good Times" would never end. They had no concerns about the Government stealing the fruits of the producer's labor. This "leveling of the playing field" or "spreading the wealth around" was used to bribe the Takers and keep them firmly on the ideological reservation. The economic tipping point occurred when the number of Takers greatly outnumbered the Producers. This insured the Progressives with a political majority. Now with total control of the government, the Progressives finally could reveal their hidden agenda to fundamentally transform America into their image. Their agenda had to be hidden until the time was right, because the Progressives knew the honest, hard working, God-Fearing Citizens would reject their ideology. In the past they worked slow but steady, implementing their Progressive takeover of America. This task was made easier by the enabling old main line news media. In early 2009, no one could stop the Progressive hostile takeover of America. Now it was clear the "emperor had no clothes". The Progressive Elite no longer hid in the shadows and gutter of society. Now with a firm grip on the throats of Americans, their will was to be done!

As the government and economy collapsed, the Leftist knew nothing but the antics of their olds ways. The progressives took to the streets to protest and demand social justice. In the City of New York, Al Sharpton and his megaphone orchestrated a small demonstration. As in the past, CNN, NBC, CNBC and other leftist media were present to record every moment with delight. Al led the chats, WHAT DO WE WANT, SOCIAL JUSTICE, WHEN DO WE WANT IT, NOW. This mindless chant went on for several minutes, until a large group of people approached the protestors. Al screamed in horror saying" run for your lives, they are the "Takers". By then it was too late, the Takers had stripped Al of his Italian handmade leather shoes, his finely tailored pin striped silk suit and all his "bling". He now stood there, alone in the middle of the street wearing only his slightly soiled shorts. His face had fallen, ash in color. He looked up towards heaven and said. " My God, My God, what have I done"? Before this occurred, the media support had faded away. No one was there to record his disgrace. All he had left of value was his gold teeth.

Other former Progressive leaders and 'Racial Pimps" fared no better. Once a menace to society, Jesse Jackson (JJ) was no longer a player. A severe shortage of Viagra forced JJ to realize that he could have no more children, in or out of wedlock. He was saddened since "he could no longer rise to the occasion". These terrible times have forced morality on some people. Jessie could no longer blackmail companies over racial issues, since few companies were left. He was still surrounded by young willing women but could never again enjoy the delicacy of their youth.

Some time ago, JJ and Big Al crusaded for the just cause to end racial injustice. This placed them in the spotlight and made them very wealthy. Soon the cause for racial equality became more about their power and prestige. The European-Americans tried to make financial and social amends for the racist actions of their forefathers. JJ and Big Al had to stoke the dying ember of racism, trying to make it an eternal flame. Without the just cause against racism, they would be nothing but average rich middle aged African-Americans. They looked for racism at every nook and cranny. Racism became harder and harder to find in society. The attention showered upon them began to fade. They even supported radical Latino protest and marches in Arizona in May 2010. How could a sovereign state attempt to control immigration? They went everywhere looking high and low for racism. It must exist somewhere? They were shocked when after an exhaustive search; a racist was found in their reflection, while looking in a mirror. How could they protest or blackmail themselves. There was now no money or fame to be gained from the poverty and racial pimp business. The Television Cameras were long gone and with no microphones in sight, they retired to the rocking chairs on their front porch.

Many years ago in Ancient Europe, there was a young boy living in a small village at the edge of a great primeval forest. Being bored and mischievous, he thought of playing a trick on the gullible town folk. He went into the forest and hid, calling as loudly as he could "Wolf, Wolf". The town folk came running with pitchforks in hand. They soon realized it was a false alarm. Several days passed and the little boy again hid in the woods and called "Wolf, Wolf". Again the town folks came running into the woods but this time upon seeing nothing, they became angry for being tricked. Many days elapsed and the little boy was playing alone in the woods. There he saw a viscous looking wolf heading towards him. The wolf neared, his teeth snarling and making a frightful growl. The boy, shaking due to fear, called out "Wolf, Wolf". The wolf closed upon the boy until they were face to snout. The town folk would not be tricked again, and the wolf pounced on the little boy and ate him alive.

Flash forward to the present day. The racial pimps holler "Racism, Racism". The people came with great urgency to the scene of the hate crime, but found no evidence. This scene was repeated so often, that people no longer responded to the cry. The racial pimps uttered Racism so often that it's meaning was blurred and lost significance. It was later used if you disagreed with any views of the pimps. Even truth uttered from the all Mighty God if conflicted with the thinking of the race pimps, would be called racist. Reading and speaking certain words of God as recorded in the Bible were considered hate speech.

It's like going on a long tedious journey for racial equality. Once you arrive at the destination, you are unclear what to do next. Your whole existence and being was entrenched in the moment. Once equality was realized, you are forced admit most of your failures in life were due to your shortcomings and lack of personal responsibility. The "Takers" were lost and confused. The government could no longer support them, and they lacked someone to blame.

With the economic destruction of the country, even Bill Clinton had remorse. All the McDonald's across the land had closed, ending his love affair with the Big Mac. Premium foot long hand rolled Cuba Cigars were impossible to find at any price. Former President Clinton now realized that cigars should never be used for anything except smoking. He wishes he had the cigars wasted in the Monica Affair. He now was sorry for re-defining the meaning of sex. "I did not have sex with that woman". This perverse play on words is known as the "Clinton - Lewinsky Effect". In a fetal position, a fake tear rolled down his chubby rosy cheek.

Upon of hearing that her millions of dollars of investments made from special insider deals were now worthless, Hillary flew into a rage lasting for days. To complicate matters, D size alkaline forever lasting batteries could no longer be found. She sent the Secret Service to search far and wide, but they returned without success. For their failure, Hillary gave them a tongue-lashing that lasted for days. Her battery-operated friend, "Mrs. Happy", would never be the same. Hillary wearing a pale blue pantsuit stood silently for countless hours staring out the front window of her New York Mansion. No one knew what ran through her mind. In late 2010 as the popularity of the Democratic Party declined with the American People, in particular their leader, Hillary enacted her plan to challenge Barack in the next presidential election. She schemed and laid in waiting like a lioness waiting to pounce when the moment was right. Bill Clinton and many of her former comrades like James Carville discreetly plotted to overthrow the sitting President at the ballot box. Hillary was emotionally devastated when she again lost the Democratic primary vote to de-throne President Obama. Her main desire in life, being President, would never be fulfilled. She regretted challenging and losing again to Barack Obama during the Democratic Primary of 2012. Barack had a lock on the Black vote and support of the Associated Progressive Press and Associated Progressive Media. Bill and Hillary had always had their support in the past. This attempt for the Presidency forever ended her political ambitions.

It was not all her fault, Bill had not been more than a political husband for many years, as she was a wife. The Secret Service detail without payment for several weeks, gladly left the Clinton's to fend for their families. At least they were well armed and removed from the acid tongue of Hillary.

Europe lads the Way

The Maastricht Treaty signed on November 1, 1993 formed the European Union. Its intention was to create a single economic market, standardize laws and regulations. This allowed the free movement of people, goods and services. Europe now had a means to equal the economic clout of the United States.

The crippling disease of Socialism struck first and was most contagious in Europe. This disease was later spread by Progressives into the United States. The 28 members of the European Union (EU) is as follows: Austria, Belgium, Bulgaria, Cyprus, Czech Republic, Denmark, Estonia, Finland, France, Germany, Greece, Hungary, Ireland, Italy, Latvia, Lithuania, Luxembourg, Malta, Netherlands, Poland, Portugal, Romania, Slovakia, Slovenia, Spain, Sweden, Turkey and the United Kingdom. The italicized member countries were in 2010 already near the tipping point of financial disaster.

This highlights the failure of Socialism wherever it is applied. Many nations of the EU also had the policy of "Give everybody a Home". They quickly followed the American example of sub-prime home lending. Again my motto applies: "Crap in, crap out". Progressive Europeans with their eight weeks paid vacation, universal health care and cradle to the grave entitlement mentality led the world into economic and political abyss. Emptying the treasury and titanic size budget deficits was a short-term prescription for appeasement with terrible and devastating side effects. Live for today and let someone else worry about tomorrow. One can delay the inevitable, but one day your problems will "come home to roost".

The most financially stable European Counties like Germany and Great Britain tried to bail out the troubled EU countries. This lending of billions of Euros and the subsequent default of these loans, hasten the demise of all members of the EU. The weakness of the Euro, made the hapless dollar temporarily seem like a better investment. The United States gave billions of borrowed dollars to the International Monetary Fund (IMF). This fund attempted to stabilize Europe's monetary system. This money loaned by the IMF came with "strings attached" The government employee unions and progressives in countries like Greece would not accept the austerity measures. This meant higher taxes and reduced pay and benefits for government workers and those receiving entitlements. Many Progressive Greek Radicals began to protest and riot. This social unrest slowly crept across the Atlantic. Separated by great oceans would no longer provide protection from the world's economic and political woes. Great Britain had to shorten its name to only "Britain". Sixteen of the member states shared the Euro as the common currency. These countries now had something worthless in common.

I have always admired the people of Great Britain. Several years back their Progressive Government confiscated the weapons from its citizens. My question is: "What are you going to do, when the Takers come for you". The land of my forefathers at the end of government will be a barren wasteland. Had only they re elected Winston Churchill as prime minister after WW2. A conservative leader would slow the destructive ways of the socialist. His defeat at the polls ushered in the Progressives. Nothing more needs to be said!

"Them Chicken's are coming home to Roost"

Our founding fathers with wisdom from God created a near perfect union in 1776. These leaders had great clarity of thought, character, morality and personal convictions. They believed in the betterment of mankind over their own interest and ambitions. Had our founding fathers lost the Revolutionary War, they and their families would have lost everything, including up to their lives.

Today most of our politicians are interested in what maintains or increases their prestige, power and wealth. At the close of the Constitutional Convention of 1787, Benjamin Franklin was queried as he left Independence Hall on the final day of deliberation. He was asked, "Well, Doctor, what have we got - a Republic or a Monarchy?" Franklin replied "A Republic, if you can keep it". Webster's Dictionary defines the word "Republic as "a political order in which the supreme power is held by a body of citizens who are entitled to vote for officers and representatives responsible to them.
Many current political leaders answer to no one!

Democracy is defined as "Government exercised either directly by the people or through elected representatives.

The following quote is attributed to Alexander Fraser Tytler (1747-1813):

A democracy cannot exist as a permanent form of government. It can only exist until the voters discover that they can vote themselves largesse from the public treasury. From that moment on, the majority always votes for the candidates promising the most benefits from the public treasury with the result that a democracy always collapses over loose fiscal policy, always followed by a dictatorship. The average age of the world's greatest civilizations has been 200 years.

Great nations rise and fall. The people go from bondage to spiritual truth, to great courage, from courage to liberty, from liberty to abundance, from abundance to selfishness, from selfishness to complacency, from complacency to apathy, from apathy to dependence, from dependence back again to bondage.

The above wordy writing of Alexander Tytler is near Biblical in meaning. This prophecy had to be written for this time of the History of the United States. Now it is clear why I titled the book "The Next to Last American President". By the end of two thousand and twelve, "Takers" comprised part of a political majority that voted always for the Progressives. The Progressives kept the "Takers" fat and happy on the social justice reservation until the end. To maintain their eternal patronage, Government would never take short-term pain to ensure long-term gain. In essence many of our national political leaders and citizens lived for the present, and let the future be damned. Once politicians with the backing of their supporters pried open the massive doors and looted the treasury, it created such euphoria that all financial restraint was lost. Later these politicians claimed to be temporarily insane. We lived for the moment, and that time has come. Creating a looming severe financial calamity and denying the inevitable will only hasten disaster and worsen the outcome.

Many people were conditioned by the Progressives that problems in life were never their fault. Someone else must be responsible! Government existed to ease the burdens of life with a never-ending flow of money and services. I experienced this recently with the flooding in Nashville Tennessee in May 2010. Federal Emergency Management Agency (FEMA) dispensed checks to many in need. Even displaced homeless people, who lived under a bridge, received a check from FEMA for $4,000 since their tent city was flooded. After cashing their government checks at "Check a Matic", local liquor stores had a sales bonanza. Stolen shopping carts loaded to the brim with merchandise were seen rolling back to the tent city under a bridge along the banks of the Cumberland River. The residents of Tent City could now afford clean underwear. Another problem with being generous with others people's wealth is the Federal Government ran a budget deficit of One Trillion, nine hundred Billions dollars for the budget year of Two Thousand and Ten. Did the recipient of government gratis care about the negative future outcome of this spending? Answer - No. But the day of reckoning was quickly approaching.

When you were young, your mother and/or father would soothe you when you scraped you knee or had other problems. If you were hungry, mom would provide food.

The Federal Government became a substitute for mom and dad and personal responsibility. This became a multi generational cradle to grave welfare state. A major problem arose after government got people addicted to government services, and then went into receivership. The withdrawal pains were horrifying for many.

2 Timothy 3:1 This know also, that in the last days perilous times shall come.

October 1, 2012

Day 1- China, Japan and Saudi Arabia would not longer loan US Money to sustain the debt and reckless spending. The Chinese Premier rebuked Obama for not heeding the prior request for financial sanity.

Day 2- The Dow Jones sustained a 1500-point drop in value in one day. President Obama called for an investigation. He knew that he could never be responsible! Where was George W. Bush?

Day 3 - Citizens and foreign governments began to question the valuation of the American Paper Currency. The Dollar began to fall on the world markets.

Day 4 - Banks ceased making loans, and began to call in every loan possible.

Day 5 - Moody's Bond Rating Service downgraded the status of US bonds and other financial obligations below junk bond status.

Day 6 - The treasury was forced to offer interest rate of 39%, if anyone would buy bonds. This created hyper-super dooper inflation.

Day 7 - President Obama was live on national media saying" all we have to fear is fear itself" he further added "I am The One, my presence and voice will cure all financial ills". Even his daughters began to snigger.

Day 8 - People everywhere dumped their dollars as fast as possible. Spending every last cent on food, fuel and survival supplies. Phone lines were hopelessly jammed with calls to 1-866- Gold Line. The selling of gold ceased when Gold Line determined they were selling something of value for near worthless currency.

If you had money, it had to be spent, because it's buying power reduced daily. The stock market ceased functioning on March 14, 2013. The ticker tape was now silent. Any investment based upon the dollar was worthless. Land, particularity that used for farming, had value although no longer based in dollars. This land could produce essential agricultural products in great demand for bartering and survival. Pasture supported grazing animals such as cows, sheep and miniature horses. The only problem is that farmers needed money or credit to purchase fuel, equipment, seeds and fertilizer. How could these items be purchased without money or credit? The answer initially would be gold, silver and other precious metals. Those with gold could make loans to farmers for a percentage of the crop. At harvest time the farmers after repaying the loans bartered for needed goods or services with excess crops.

The entire economy of the United States was based upon the "Dollar" being the medium of exchange. Workers were paid for their labor with Dollars; the senior citizens retirement income was based on dollars. Even the "Takers" were bribed with Dollars. Every product or service purchased was paid in Dollars. I hate to inform you that the dollar will be nevermore!
If you were fortunate in the past to be worth millions of dollars on paper, it would not be worth the paper it is written. This includes certificates of deposits, money market, stock's and bonds.

How could a company sell its products? With what means will the employees be compensated? Government at the Federal Level continued in a reduced form as long as it had gold reserves. President Obama, now in a panic stands with his Progressive Friends on a street corner in Chicago, passing out twenty dollars gold pieces to the "Takers". They lined up for miles to receive gratis. Takers were elated to receive "Obama's stash", but felt the gloom settling over the country. The depression deepened since the Progressives could not change, destroying the nation in the final orgy of spending, redistributing the producer's wealth to their perceived rightful owners.

The radical Islamic Terrorist who lived only to destroy America and its economy, were furious that their brother, Barack Hussien Obama, had destroyed America, cheating them of revenge. How will they earn their 70 virgins in the after life? They lost their sure fire ticket to their paradise. The terrorist wandered aimlessly searching for someone else to hate. The Islamic Terrorist would never refer to America as the "Great Satan". We became one of many "Little Satan's"

As my wife tells me timing is everything! The following advice is worth ten thousand times the price of this book, adjusted for the dollar value in 2013. Right before the economic crash, borrow as much money as possible. Use this money to buy land, a BMW 760 Li ($124,000), armored vehicle, gold and tons of survival supplies. Say you borrowed one million dollars and then come the crash of the economy and the demise of the Federal Government. Later you can pay back the loan with nearly worthless dollars. What a deal! In 2010 if you bought 40 ounces of gold at 1200 dollars per ounce. Wait until after the economic collapse in early 2013, the gold is now worth $25,000 per ounce. The 40 ounces of gold purchased for $48,000 in 2010 is now worth a million dollars in 2013. What a great rate of return! Redeem the gold for dollars; pay off all your debts and look good driving the BMW 760 Li.

I borrowed money from a local Bank several years ago to build a home. At that time money was something of value. After 2013, I can repay the loan with nearly worthless U.S. hundred dollar bills. Then I will call the Dave Ramsey Show (if it still exists) and shout, "I am debt free". You probably could find wads of hundred dollar bills just lying around, particularity around the bodies of former millionaires who jumped from a penthouse suite. With hyper super duper inflation in the next few years, I might be making $500,000 annually by the end of 2013. This will equal the buying power of $100,000 in 2010 dollars. My home loan is not adjusted for inflation, so paying the fixed monthly note will not be a problem. This also assumes I have a job. Unfortunately the prices of other items will inflate. A store brand loaf of bread will cost $75 US.

One adverse thought about the impending economic collapse is my life insurance. If I wait to die until 2014, my wife collecting on my life insurance would be paid in worthless dollars. This would assume that the insurance company is still around. If this book doesn't sell, maybe I should check out early. I thought for many years I was worth more dead than alive. In three years this might be a mute point.

This is a similar procedure that President Obama plans to repay our trillions in loans to Foreign Countries. It's only fair; we borrowed the money in dollars and will repay the loans with dollars. It could not be his fault the money is nearly worthless. The Federal Treasury printing presses are printing hundred bills around the clock. I don't think the Chinese will accept this accommodation.

Unless you are repaying old loans, dollars are useless. You initially could buy repossessed property, pre owned BMW'S, yachts, etc by buying the now worthless loans from mortgage companies and banks. This is assuming there remain any financial institutions. The banks will repossess so many vehicles; they lacked lots to store all the vehicles. I shed a tear when my favorite bank teller "Angie" lost her job when the bank closed. Occasionally while fuel was available, I would drive to her old drive thru window just to reminisce.

Without jobs and money, the population had no means to buy food, much less payback-borrowed money. In the near future the unemployment rate reached 90%, with few companies remaining.

Hospitals will fail; most doctors close their offices. They had no means to pay rent, employees or purchase supplies. Medical research and development ceased without funding. We could no longer subsidize the medical care of the world. It's a shame that we never found a cure for the common cold. Your health insurance company sadly tried to reimburse medical providers with dollars. Before the hospitals closed, an older man desperate for medical care went to the emergency room complaining of chest pains. He was told the hospital was closing today, due to the economic crisis and could not help him. He said I can pay, and pulled from his pocket a thick wad of hundred-dollar bills. Once in days past he was very wealthy. The hospital emergency room clerk sadly said, "That money is now worthless". All the medical staff already had been let go. Rejected, the old man went home to die.

Many millions will perish from a shortage of medicine. The "Rebound Effect" from abruptly ending maintenance medication will doom many. It is a shame that my doctor will not prescribe a years supply of medicine at a time. I fear most of all not having access to antibiotics. A minor sinus infection without treatment could lead to a horrible death. I would miss the hours spent waiting to see my Doctor. Those now were remembered fondly as the good ole days.

The fancy high tech medical devices were of little value when the electrical grid failed. Hospitals had backup diesel generators, which kept them operational until the diesel supplies were exhausted. With the dollar worthless, there were no means to buy fuel. Many doctors volunteered medical services until supplies and medicine was depleted. Universal Health Care was to begin in 2014. This now consisted of an aspirin and a used Q-tip.

Imagine a country in which government offers no public assistance!
No social security, Medicare, Medicaid, food, housing, education and of course, no healthcare, universal or not. It was my luck as I approached retirement; there was no retirement, either private or public.
All pension and retirement income is never more. Past sources of income from savings, certificate of deposit, bonds, stocks, pension, and social security were gone with the economy. If you could find food, by what means can it be bought? Do you have anything of value to barter or trade? How do you like all the Treasury bills and bonds? It was a tragedy that Obama and his fellow progressives forced the public to place all their retirement wealth into government bonds. That was change, for the worse!

There will be a massive famine in America, the like never seen even in Africa. Tens of thousands will perish daily due to starvation, disease and ever increasing violence. Many will take a life for a grain of rice. We were in such need that food assistance was requested from other countries. Our pleas for help were met with scorn. For countless generations we were the most generous country in the history of mankind. We gave billions upon billions to most of the African continent and other third world nations. When we desperately needed aid none was forthcoming. The famine in the third world countries devastated the population. They lived at the edge of existence barely surviving even with our foreign aid. We could no longer feed them.

Those individuals who listened and could obey my mentor Glen Beck, faired much better during the economic collapse. They bought gold, survival food and non-hybrid seeds enough to grow a one-acre survival garden. I can already taste the freshly harvested squash and green beans. For city folks, you are screwed since a garden will not grow on asphalt. As been previously stated, "What are you going to do when the "Takers" come for you"? You must be well armed and have the constitution to defend your family and property. The Progressives were such "caring people" never owning a weapon and were concentrated in large cities. With no means of defense or place to hide they will be largely wiped out early in the insurrection. They were at their best while spending other people's money. No wealth left to confiscate, nothing could be redistributed to its rightful owners. Having lost their quest for social justice, the remaining progressives quietly vanished from the great cities, just as with the Mayan Culture. At least something good came from this devastation.

Total and absolute despair gripped the country. People in large cities such as New York and Chicago faired the worst. The cities became a cesspool of starvation, lawlessness and utter hopelessness. All public services as water, electricity, sanitation, police and firefighters began to break down and finally ceased to function. For a brief time a few workers in these areas continue to work without pay, until the Union Bosses proclaimed all work to cease immediately. They were ordered by the union bosses to join a picket line and protest. This protest was short lived due to growing violence and no news media or onlookers left to witness the gathering. The protestors joined a mass exodus of city dwellers without purpose, searching everywhere for food and shelter. There were no jobs, no real money and no hope.

Psalms 11:2-3 For, lo, the wicked bend their bow, they make ready their arrow upon the string, that they may privily shoot at the upright in heart. If the foundations were destroyed, what can the righteous do?

Most Illegal Immigrants went home to Mexico and where ever. There were no jobs left for them to take from Americans, no free education, housing, and healthcare. They became hostile when their government food debit cards were denied at the grocery store and casinos. This rejection caused riots in every major city. No media was left to cover their protest and no one else giving a Damn. The ignored protestors finally gave up, packed their belongings and headed home. Their last act in America was to steal everything that would fit into their pickups. They broke into grocery, gun and jewelry stores. New extended cab pickups were even stolen off the truck dealer's showroom. The dust cloud from their vehicles heading south, reminded some of scenes from the "Dust Bowl". Americans living near the border with Mexico tried to follow and flee with the immigrants back to Mexico. Mexico unlike America strictly enforced its borders and immigration laws. The Americans trying to flee into Mexico were robbed of their last possessions, beaten by the Mexican Border Guards, and told by penalty of death never again to attempt to cross the border. The captured "Gringos" had a small Mexican Flag tattooed on their forehead. This mark would identify them for termination if they again crossed the border. An American Progressive young woman with bare breasts, pleaded with the guards to let her family cross into Mexico. She said: "What of all the years we supported your people crossing the border into America and freely gave them our country". A grisly disheveled Mexican border guard replied in broken English; "We Mexicans are not stupid like you gringos, we took and took from your country, now it is gone" he then said, "You will not take from us as we did you".

I recently watched the TV Show "Border Wars." This is definitely not a war! The illegal's swim and run, with US Border Guards in pursuit. A prison style fence with razor wire along the border would solve most of illegal border crossings. If this is a "war," where are the Apache Helicopters? Had we enforced our borders the country might have survived? At least without this social and financial burden there would be several more years to upright the sinking economic ship of state. Listed below are "Pros and Cons" of illegal immigration:

Pros	Cons
Cheap labor	Depress wages and take American Jobs
Take over of California	None
Votes for Progressives	Destroys integrity of elections
Increased sales of used trucks	More uninsured drivers
Increase police employment	Increased crime and gangs
Make slumlords money	Slums
Social safety valve for Mexico	Their problem is now our problem!
Pleasing pot heads	Drug cartels and violence
Jobs for Immigration lawyers	More lawyers
Increased real estate related jobs	Mortgage Loan Fraud
Good authentic Mexican Food	Heartburn
increased liquor sales	Drunken Illegal's, American road kill
None	entitlement spending into oblivion

Many undocumented immigrants brought more that them selves illegally into this country. AIDS originated many years ago in Africa. An African was infected while doing something with a monkey. This politically correct disease crossed the border and spread across America. This dread disease would not been the problem if we had a "one man, one woman" social contract. One gets always in trouble when your path is away from God. Remember the unintended consequences of Europeans arrival in the "New World", bringing diseases which the native population had no resistance. I greatly admire and miss the Native Americans. The remaining vestigial natives never returned to their former greatness.

Some old timers remember the classic Christmas Song "Chestnuts roasting on an open fire". What are they singing about; there are no chestnut trees in America. A Chinese immigrant variety of the tree entered the country carrying a fungus deadly to our trees. Our native population with no resistance to the new pest was decimated. It was told that up to one billion chestnut trees perished.

To all the employers who knowingly employed Illegal Immigrants, payback will be Hell! They give all the typical excuses:

1. They take jobs that Americans won't do.
2. Mexicans work harder
3. Mexicans are more reliable
4. They don't report injuries as often
5. Illegal's work for less money
6. Don't complain as much, at least in English
7. Better fence climbers
8. They don't commit crimes in my fancy neighborhood
9. They automatically replace themselves.
10. Makes the greedy employers mucho money.

Every dollar earned by an illegal immigrant requires a subsidy of two dollars from the legal native population. (Reference-Me) We would be better off to pay them to stay in Mexico. Listed below is some of the social and financial cost of illegal immigration:

1. Crime - murder, rape, robbery, assault without a battery, shoplifting.
2. Cost of educating their children
3. Expense of border lack of protection
4. Room and board while in prison, room and board out of prison
5. Universal Latino Healthcare
6. DUI'S - killed and mutilate thousands of Americans while driving drunk.
7. Free all you can eat nachos and other grocery items.
8. Government paid cellular phone with unlimited calls to Mexico
9. Drugs and the associated violence, gangs and drug lords.
10. Vote for Progressives.

"Country Livin, Is The Life For Me"

I live in a beautiful place in harmony with nature. We have mature towering oaks reaching towards the sky. There are deer, wild turkeys and other birds galore.

Speaking of Turkeys:

1. Benjamin Franklin stated Turkeys should be the national bird. I agree with Ben on this matter. Turkey's and people have much in common. All tom turkeys that get lucky with the hens and forty percent of males who impregnate women are alike, since they are nothing but sperm donors. I would further say that hens are smarter than their human counterparts in many ways. A hen turkey makes the toms strut their stuff and display his wares. A Hen decides what Tom she will mate based upon the Tom's genetic and physical fitness. Not any Tom will get the primeval prize!

    After mating the tom turkey abandon the hens until the next season. At least for most of the year he is not hen-pecked. A tom turkey is basically good for only three things; eating, mating, and for me to watch especially during the mating season when they are displaying for the ladies. A mature healthy Tom Turkey in love is a beautiful sight!

    I thank God for his blessings for allowing my family to live here. This wonderful place on earth can never compare to the next everlasting one that God has prepared. I pray that my family can reside here for many years!

Having five acres of land, I could grow a garden and perhaps raise a few head on miniature cattle. The smaller version of cattle would require less food and space and fit easier in my freezer (if we had electricity). Without electricity you could form a cooperative with like-minded neighbors to share perishable food items. I would love to have some miniature horses on my mini-farm. I will wait to see how the country goes. Europeans that were starving during World War Two were forced to develop a taste for horse.

The people living in the rural areas have a better chance of survival. This brought to mind a Country Song written by Hank Williams Jr.:

A COUNTRY BOY CAN SURVIVE (Abbreviated)

I live back in the woods you see
I've got a shotgun, a rifle
And a four wheel drive

I can plow a field all day long
I can catch catfish from dusk till dawn
Make our own whiskey
And our own smoke too
Ain't too many these ol' boys can't do
Including bocephis

We grow good ol' tomatoes
And homemade wine

Cause you can't starve us out
And you can't make us run
We say grace
And we say ma'am
If you ain't into that we don't give a damn

We came from the West Virginia coalmines
And the Rocky Mountains and the western skies

I had a good friend in New York City
He never call me bocephus
Called me hillbilly
Really

But he was killed by a man with a switchblade knife
For forty three dollars my friend lost his life
Now this dude's gonna get out in a year or two
'Cause the system don't work for me and you

we're from north California
And south alabam"
And little town all around this land

And a country boy can survive
Country Folk can survive

This poetic masterpiece written in nineteen hundred and ninety nine is even more relevant now and in the near future. It could be re titled "A country boy can survive 2013".

Having farming and grazing land would be a great asset, especially for the hard times to come. NOTE: Rich people in New York and other large cities should buy a country home with acreage. When times become perilous, you need an escape plan and a place to flee. In the future this country estate will be worth multiple times any penthouse suite. A fancy penthouse suite will become nothing more than a death trap. This brought to mind the cinematic masterpiece of director John Carpenter, "Escape from New York" (1981).

Please buy my book and may God be with you! It's time to make an investment in my Livelihood. Step up, have some "skin in the game"

I have known for some time the depression of depressions was near and wish better preparations were made. Why had I not listened to Dave Ramsey years ago? My immediate goals to prepare for the future:

1. Become debt free
2. Place a security fence around my property to keep animals in and out.
3. Have a "Glen Beck" supply of gold.
4. Buy a gas station for future needs.
5. The electrical grid will fail! Go green and generate and store electricity from solar or wind power.
6. Drill water well for future water needs.
7. Store several tons of fertilizer
8. Be armed to the teeth.
9. Buy a diesel whole house generator with 30,000 gallons of fuel.
10. Many years worth of seeds for a survival garden.
11. Ton's and Ton's of yummy survival food.
12. Rivers equivalent of bottle water in one-gallon plastic containers.
13. A compact Kubota diesel tractor with a front-end loader attachment to carry crap.
14. Armored 4 by 4 vehicle with a cattle catcher.
15. A year's supply of Hershey's 60% cacao dark chocolate in the 3.52 ounce size or larger.
16. A year's supply of prescription medicine
17. 25 pairs of Khaki size 50 "St. Johns Bay" relaxed fit slacks
18. Cases and cases of "Little Debbie" snack cakes for my wife
19. 500 pounds of Beneful Weight Reduction dog food for our sweetie "Nora".
20. Have Sarah Palin for personal protection. I feel safer already!

Mitt's Too Late

President Obama ran for re-election in 2012. The Republican opponent was Mitt Romney. The ship of state was slowly sinking for some time due to the increasing weight of deficit spending. The former captain of the ship, Barack Obama said open the hatches and full steam ahead with Government spending. He must at all risk speed up the re distribution of wealth since he probably would only have one term as president. This caused the ship of state to take on the waters of deficit spending four times faster than his predecessor George W. Bush. At the end of Obama's first and only presidential term, the ship of state was listing far to the left. Deficit waters were pouring in the open portholes and hatches. Even small economic waves were now topping the deck. One larger economic wave would cause the entire country to capsize. Even his dream of being a socialist dictator was quickly fading. Obama tried without success to suspend the election due to a national emergency - HIM. By the time of the presidential election on November 4, 2012, the Federal Government of the United States had all but disintegrated.

Mitt Romney won the election is a landside. Even though President Obama provided citizenship and the immediate right to vote to all the illegal aliens in the country prior to the election, their ten million votes were not enough. Mitt Romney was the 45th and last President of the United States.

I never forgave him for Romney Care in Massachusetts. The idea of Universal Healthcare is noble, but government implementation is the problem. This was a constitutional right given to the states, not the federal government. His inauguration in January 2013 was a bleak affair. Mitt Romney had won the race, but the prize was already spent. He sat alone day after day in the Former White House with little to do.

The long awaited day for Obama's nationalized healthcare had arrived. People lined up in front of their local emergency rooms for their free healthcare. Unfortunately this massive new entitlement became effective as bankruptcy folded the country. Many stood in line as hospitals closed their doors. This created riots and great despair. Was not free comprehensive health care a guaranteed right under the constitution?

President Romney was often seen around the grounds of White House. During the spring and summer, he was outdoors riding the John Deere 997 Diesel Z Trac Zero turn mower. Mrs. Romney stayed busy helping with the cooking and cleaning. The rent-a-cop at the front gate was occupied receiving wreaths and condolences on the demise of the country. Mounds of flowers were deposited along the fence and sidewalk on the front side of the White House. Russia and China's wreaths were enormous and left with great joy. The White House Fence was now electrified to keep people either in or out. In reality, Mit Romney became the President of the District of Columbia. That's a job that no one in his or her right mind would want! He stated" I spent millions of dollars and two years campaigning for this"!

Many companies and the jobs they provided had vanished by early 2013. I still had my small business, although customers could no longer pay for my service. As the customer base dwindled, so did my income. What income left was paid in dollars! Gee Thanks! I came to work day after day as always before, but with no electricity, phone or computer, I decided to retreat to the home place. After all, the back porch was awaiting me. I could always cut firewood, haul water, raise a garden, tend to the livestock and listen to my wife.

One of the businesses missed more than Kroger's, was McDonald's. Monday through Friday for 52 weeks a year I was a regular morning customer at the drive thru. My large coffee with 2 creams and five equal, Sausage McMuffin and small water cost $2.19 in 2010. The price had risen to $4.90 by July 2011 and $12.99 by the end of 2012. By the start of 2013, the once thriving business closed. Even though fuel was expensive and in short supply, I made it to the McDonalds "Going out of business Sale". It was a bittersweet day. The last Sausage McMuffin melted in my mouth. For years to come, all that remained was the memory of that moment. A tear ran down the cheek of Ronald McDonald, making a mess of his well-applied makeup.

This business failure was not the fault of the McDonalds Corporation or the local franchise owner. The free enterprise system and capitalism were the optimum economic system. This functioned best without the impediment of government burdensome regulations and taxation. The Federal Government with Progressive Policies destroyed this once great country. Politicians appeasing their constituency raided the treasury, and forced excessive regulation and taxation upon the teeming masses. The famous quote of Alexander Tytler came to fruition with the last progressive reign of terror. Never again would I taste and hold the McMuffin. No longer will my taste buds have such a treat. The Sausage McMuffin taken with a large hot delicious cup of coffee was a great way to start your morning. McDonalds, taps are playing for you! Ronald McDonald the clown was laid off only to work the occasional kid's birthday parties. To me that clown was always a little scary. The Happy Meal toys will be missed!

The Rule of the "Takers"

The inner nature of the "Takers" once partially controlled by the police, prisons and bribery by the Federal Government, was now fully unleashed. They were free to rape and pillage without regard to consequence. The righteous trembled in fear, dreading what nightfall may bring. Anything of value the "Takers' wanted was almost free for the taking. This was most frightening in the major cities that had banned the ownership of guns by the law-abiding middle class. The Takers once only ruined the inner cities eventually took over most large metropolitan areas and later tried to invade the suburbs and the rural areas.

At first the "Takers" rioted and broke into local grocery, electronics, and liquor and "bling" stores. The home improvement stores were initially spared since they sold items intended for working people. The infrastructure began to fail due to age and lack of maintenance. There were nothing of real value to pay for the production and transmission of electricity. Without electricity, the stolen 52" high definition 3-D television sets were nothing more that a paper weight. Cable and satellite television providers went out of business even before the end of electricity. It was a colorful site at night to watch the satellites lose orbit and fall back to the earth. As it has been said "what goes up must come down". Before electricity failed "Takers" had spent countless hours watching static. They still carried the Government paid cell phones, and acted like they were talking to someone.

With the total breakdown of society, them "Takers" were free, free at last. They now supremely ruled the inner cities. Every imaginable vice was available for the taking. The ancient peoples of Sodom and Gomorrah would have been shocked by their crimes against man and nature. The Bible partially describes their actions in Romans1: 29-31.

Being filled with all unrighteousness, fornication, wickedness, covetousness, maliciousness; full of envy, murder, debate, deceit, malignity; whisperers, Backbiters, haters of God, despiteful, proud, boaster, inventor of evil things, disobedient to parents, Without understanding, covenant-breaker, without natural affection, implacable, unmerciful.

The Bible as always, flows with Godly wisdom. The inspired words of God are recorded in the greatest history book, the Bible. Its divine message was a guide for spiritual and physical conduct in the present, past and future. The Bible accurately predicts future events that are too horrible to mention.

Please note that the Takers will not bite your back, unless they are very hungry or doing some crazy sex act. Many people faced starvation during the end of America; however reports of cannibalism were rare. To survive people resorted to actions seemingly impossible to conceive.
The "Takers" were now masters of their domain. At first they had ample supplies of stolen goods. Electrical service eventually failed, along with water, sanitation, postal delivery and natural gas. Un-natural gas remained only in limited supply. The police and firefighters even when still being paid, would not venture into areas occupied by the "Takers", for it was now too dangerous.

Many "Takers" still waited for the welfare check that always came at the first of each month. They waited for days, month after month, for the government gratis that was no more. Had a check arrived, it was just now another worthless piece of paper. They could not understand why no one came to repair and clean their trashed apartments? Public Housing in the past meant never having to say you're sorry! Someone from the Housing Authority repaired whatever he or she destroyed or trashed. The hygiene problems became so dire, that houses not yet trashed were found and occupied. Rent was free as before. The commodes were used over and over again, but without water they could not be flushed. The "Takers" were slow to understand that turning the lever on the commode doesn't mean it will flush.

Their children could not be gotten rid of during the day. There were no schools, head start centers or jungle gyms to play. This also meant their children would not receive Government paid school breakfast, lunch and dinner. There would be no free coloring books and crayons. As part of the USDA Food Program, commodities were given for free to poor people. Before the last presidential election, Michelle Obama while campaigning for Barack's re-election in Detroit was cutting up large blocks of cheese to hand out to their supporters. After her cutting of this cheese, no more was to be found. For her ten minutes of work, Michelle demanded another all expense paid trip to Spain. She was outraged being told there only enough fuel for a one way trip!

The Takers had shelter, food and clothing. If supplies ran low, they would go on another night of pillage. Food was the main concern. Clothing if needed could be collected from piles of stolen merchandise. Cadillac Escalades lined the streets, all with the best wheels and sound systems that could be stolen. Takers reasoned they were made by government motors and thus belonged to them. A major problem with their stolen vehicles is they required gasoline, which was in short supply. Searching for new resources to steal forced the "Takers" to broaden their radius of destruction, going into the unknown areas of the "Producers". They like a massive army of Soldier Ants, spreading out from the nest and cutting a wide path of destruction. Nether plants, animals or man would stand in their way. Every source of food was to be dispatched, dismembered and taken back to the hive. Any poor insect or animal in their path would be killed and completely covered in an ant feeding frenzy.

One object the "Takers" had in ample quantities was sex. This as always was a 24/7 operation. They invented new ways of having sex. I didn't think it was possible. Like basketball, they played one on one, two on one, etc. All Biblical influence was gone. Some homosexuals in the past, tried to blur the definition of marriage. This word with the "Takers' had no significance. Nine months after conceiving, a problem arose of who would raise the "Damn Children'. For generations before, they replied when asked "Yos the Daddy", the women would laughingly say "Uncle Sam". In the past, cranking out them children, meant extra in your monthly check. The "Taker" Women after a few years began to understand their welfare checks were not in the mail. Finally being forced to be responsible for your own actions put a damper on the orgy scene. Planned Parenthood was no longer a viable baby-killing machine. A pregnant Taker woman cried, "You mean I have to pay to kill this damn baby". Slowly the women learned that free and easy sex did have a heavy cost after nine months. As I have previously stated, harsh reality has forced morality on many for the first time. It is a terrible shame that the country had to be destroyed for this to occur. There is a silver lining in every dark cloud!

The "producers" were used to making their own way in life, without "Uncle Sam". The recession of 2008 and what came later was not their fault. They suffered mightily due to the Progressive emptying the treasury, borrowing US into oblivion and immoral ways. Knowing that work was not just a four-letter word, they grew gardens, traded and bartered with others for items necessary for survival. "Producer" communities banned together to provide mutual aid and assistance. This reminds of how the People in Nashville Tennessee during the flood of May 2010. After the disaster, citizens went into action, cleaning and repairing damages. Volunteers from across the area bought supplies and offered their time, money and labor. This is what is expected from a "Producer". They are an asset to the community and their fellow man. Producers ask how I can help. Takers say "where is my damn welfare, I earned it".

Contrast the flood in middle Tennessee with hurricane Katrina that hit New Orleans. The different mentality of the Producers and Takers was quite clear. The "Takers" of New Orleans were conditioned by the Progressives to let others provide cradle to the grave care. When bad times hit with Katrina, they knew nothing else but to sit on their "Asses" and wait for help. When aid arrived slower than the beneficiaries expected, they had to blame someone - GEORGE W. BUSH. Dear Progressives: "Them chickens have come home to roost".

Battle for the Cities

The Producers in the Liberal States, New York, Maine, Massachusetts, California, Oregon, Illinois, Connecticut, Maryland, New Hampshire, New Jersey, Wisconsin and Michigan fared poorly against the Takers. For the purpose of this book, the Republican States are noted as "Blue, and "Red" for the Progressive, Democratic States. The old mainline Progressive media wing of the Democratic Party reporting on national elections always had their colors reversed. "Red" is always the color associated with Communists, Socialists and Progressives.

Many of these states limited the sales and ownership of weapons by honest God fearing Americans. The Progressive politically controlled cities with the greatest Taker concentration were in years past a haven for despair, crime and urban rot. It would not take much effort to finish the destruction of cities like Detroit. When Progressives rule, people will be forced to drool. In the city of New York, it would be almost impossible to survive the end of the country. New Yorkers lacked weapons to defend themselves, and land to grow crops or graze animals. Food became scarce and New Yorkers started to starve. While supplies lasted, Spam was served by candlelight at the few remaining five star restaurants. The master chefs prepared cheesy Spam rolls, Spam salad and Spam mystery delight. Once the supplies of Spam and other tasty foods items were depleted, the chefs created new dishes. My favorite was roasted rodent seasoned with curry served over rice with red wine. At least they had clean linen tablecloths and fancy waiters. The taste of food became secondary when any food was scarce. Mayor Bloomberg was last seen sailing out of New York on his yacht. The cargo hold was filled to the brim with precious food and supplies. He raised a small crescent flag as he approached the open sea.

Asphalt and concrete jungles grew nothing but despair. Even the animals at the Bronx Zoo did not survive. A huge barbecue pit featured every animal known to man. The people remarked how ostrich tastes just like chicken. Orangutans were too tasty to just let hang around. Purina Monkey Chow was a delicacy served with Chimp Stew. The food researchers at Purina never envisioned their products used in this manner. Sloths were easy to catch since they were soooo slow. A Zoo Burger meant eating on the wild side. No zoo animal was spared, not even the elephants. How would you cook an elephant? On a giant rotisserie. The trouble with this method of cooking is that it required twelve strong men to rotate the elephant. This was the only method of cooking a whole elephant ensuring it is well done on all sides. When skewering an elephant make sure all hanging down parts like the trunk stay out of the fire. This has caused several bull elephants to spontaneously combust. This was a terrible waste of four tons of precious food! Mothers in America told their children to always clean their plates. In the past starving children in Africa were mentioned as a reason not to waste food, now it was you and your neighbors.

Starving New Yorker's asked, "How do you eat an elephant"? Many bites at a time. An elephant was made to travel; its trunk was always packed. It was told that Panda Stew was quite a taste delight. The zoo animals were in such demand that starving New Yorker's began fighting over Koala scraps.

Starvation removed all pretense of pride or importance. In this way all people were reduced to the same level in life. Was this not the goal of every Socialist for the teeming masses? They intended to punish the greedy producers by harsh taxation and regulations thus lowering their standard of living and hope for the future. Why under these conditions would the producers risk their remaining capital, hire employees to stimulate the economy. This transfer of wealth then flowed to its intended owners, the Takers. Instead of elevating the status of the Takers, all Americans were flattened.

New Yorker's who were once wealthy had the highest rate of mortality. Living in a luxury penthouse suite on the 50th floor became a deathtrap. Without electricity the elevators were nothing more than a trash chute.

If you could climb up the flight of stairs, there was no water, electricity or hope. Most of the windows in the penthouse could not be opened to allow in fresh air. During the summer the penthouse was an oven of despair. Without water, the commodes would only flush once. Some newer units had tried to install a waterless waste removal system. The Plumbing Union Bosses would have nothing of the sort. This innovation would put some union member out of work! As with all union leaders, their main concern was not their members or the general benefit of mankind, but their largess.

With so many producers packed in close proximity in a large city, they were easy to find and quickly dispatched by the Takers. There was no place to run or hide. The Progressives in the red states would not permit honest Producers to legally process weapons. The Takers never worried about laws, always had weapons and slaughtered Producers by the tens of thousands. Only the young attractive young women would be spared. They will serve as Taker Sex Slaves until their beauty faded. A river of blood flowed down Wall Street.

Fighting turned to hand to hand combat, killing at close range. Alan a Progressive tried to stop his attackers by saying "I'm one of you, a liberal Democrat ". The Takers moved closer, angrier than ever. The Progressive in sheer desperation cried "I voted for Obama". The next sounds made were never to be understood. He made only a gurgling sound as his throat was cut. The fighting continued for weeks in the streets, apartment-to-apartment and finally penthouse-to-penthouse. When the fighting ceased, the Takers took the last of the food, tons of "Bling" and thousands of supple, attractive, liberal young girls and women. Their hands bound, tied together one in front of another. The procession of woman captives, stretched for miles. The fate of the captives was more terrible than death. Unfortunately the Progressive Icon, Joy Behar did not survive. She was not young or attractive. Her loud vitriolic and profane language as the Takers neared quickly became too much for the men to bear! This vile reminded them why they were sperm donors. Their motto was: Get in, Get out and get the hell away. Well, at least Joy was a Liberal who would not be missed!

Word of the New York City Massacre slowly spread around the country. Communication became only word of mouth, spread by travelers searching for hope. When the news reached the other cities in the "Red" Progressive States, people began to panic and run into the streets. They cried: "The Takers" are coming, who will save us". They stood quietly for a moment of silence hoping for any answer. No one, not even God would answer his or her pleas. In panic gathering whatever supplies remaining, they fled the cities. Many of these people in the end will act as Takers, since they had the will, but no means to support them. They will be forced to steal and kill to survive.

They never heeded the advice of Glen Beck and his advertisers to buy gold, survival food, or non-hybrid seeds enough to grow a one acre survival garden. For many who turned a deaf ear to the prophecy of Mr. Beck, it was now too late. They never owned weapons and tried to keep others in the country from the constitutional right to bear arms. It was not all their fault, since they watched CNN, ABC, NBC, CNBC and CBS. Did they think that watching Keith Doberman would produce anything of lasting value? Besides, being a Progressive, especially a Christian Progressive made you always feel good about your self. That quest for the good feeling of social justice made one feel spiritually and morally vindicated. The best part about being a Progressive National Politician is that you never had to say "No", when spending other people's money. This created the same euphoria as shopping does for a shopaholic. The Progressive Ruling Elite and the beneficiary of the government gratis were elated until the money ran out. The terrible consequence of bankrupting the county was only contemplated and mentioned by a few patriots, one being Glen Beck.

Many never had a personal relationship with the Lord. The Progressive Christians wished that Jesus had been number one in their hearts and ministry, not social justice. For all too many, the revelation came too late. Divine peace and comfort was there for those having a personal relationship with my Lord and Savior Jesus Christ. Jesus' love and redemption for mankind is here now and for all times. Give your problems to Jesus in times of need, for he will lighten your load. God and Jesus are spiritual and everlasting. Salvation of the human race is their main concern. If one is saved, it matter's little in life if one is rich or poor, black or white. The importance of this life is preparation for the next everlasting one. That is why Jesus came to earth, born of a virgin, preached salvation, performed miracles and died on a cross. Jesus arose from an earthly death after the third day and resides forever with his heavenly father. I pray that I may be there when my short visit on earth is complete.

Romans 10 8-11 For salvation that comes from trusting Christ - which is what we preach - is already within easy reach of each of us; in fact, it is as near as our own hearts and mouths. For if you tell others with your own mouth that Jesus Christ is your Lord, and believe in your own heart that God has raised him from the dead, you will be saved. For it is believing in his heart that a man becomes right with God, and with his mouth he tells others of his faith, confirming his salvation. For the Scriptures tell us that no one who believes in Christ will ever be disappointed.

The above passage was put in the book for my "Aunt Margaret"

The Fleeing

They fled their concrete and asphalt jungles known as cities, many for the first time, regretted past liberal ways. Many people without hope moved from place to place, without direction, trying to survive another day. The end of America was most harsh on the large city dwellers. They knew little of hunting, fishing or how to grow a garden. No longer could you frequent an expensive five star restaurant. No oysters on the half shell. This business and their expensive cuisine were a tasty memory. Americans once had such abundance, eating was a pleasurable experience, just not for sustenance. Even for home consumption, most food was processed, pre cooked and ready to eat, just microwave for five minutes. We never appreciated the farmer who grew the food, the food processors, distributors, and truck drivers. The products of our desire were sold in modern supermarkets and were always there. Entering a clean, well-lit store was a pleasant experience. The grocery retailers went out of their way to make an enjoyable shopping experience. There was isle after isle of every product desired by man. To pay for these items you could use cash; write a check or swipe a credit or debit card. All of these instruments of payment were based upon the dollar being of value. When the dollar collapsed as legal tender, there was no means to trade for goods or services. At first there was only the inefficient bartering system. The country reverted in time before the industrial revolution. Most thought the technological advances of mankind would continue unabated forever. Many great ancient civilizations reached a pinnacle in cultural and scientific discovery, erecting great monuments and creating great and wondrous things. Today their buildings have cracked and crumbled. Nature totally reclaimed many of their achievements. Thoughts of their intellectuals and most of their advanced knowledge and achievements were lost over time.

Many people became so desperate they resorted to dumpster dining. Any leftover morsel of food was to be relished. Food became scarce and times worsened, no one had scraps to be discarded and no refuse company remained to empty the dumpsters. Starvation spread like an epidemic, nursing young mothers without proper nutrition stopped producing milk. Lacking baby food or mother's milk many had to endure the endless cries of hunger from their dying infants. The sight and smell of human misery and devastation was everywhere!

Staying overweight during this period was nearly impossible. If one were still pleasantly plumb, others would know you must have an ample supply of survival food. You must be a follower of the survival cult leader Glen Beck! Takers intent on redistributing your apparent wealth of food would soon visit you.

Trash now covered city sidewalks, parks and lakes. Some people lived in shanties near dumpsites. Young children were constantly combing the site for any food, metal or anything that could be re-sold for a token amount. At least people were serious about recycling.

Sewer systems in the large cities were nothing but a haven for rats. They provided valuable hunting grounds. The hunger crisis deepened when the rat population was decimated by over hunting. The sewers were also a place for the former producers to hide from the Takers.

Squatter groups largely of former city dwellers began to spring up wherever land was available. People from the Northern Cities fled on foot towards rural areas, especially to the south. Florida was always a popular retirement spot. Illegal's Immigrants undertook a reverse migration, back to their home country.

This created open hostility with their neighbors whose land and resources the "Squatters" had occupied. Survival was tedious for everyone. If you listened to past wise words of "Glen Beck" and had land for farming, your living conditions for your family would be better than most. As in the past, people who desperately needed resources resorted to force. Only a few people had enough of anything to share other than misery. This pitted local producers against the migrant ones. Desperate for survival, the migrants had no choice but to attack the locals. Again the city folk from the Red Progressive States were defeated as with the Takers. Many of the migrants were never seen again. Their rotting corpses lined the route of their retreat. This event became known as the" Second Trail of Tears". Chris Matthews never had another tingle down his leg or shed a tear thinking of Obama. Before Chris died on the trail, he cried "My God, My God, what have I done'. "I thought he was the anointed one". Many have perished following a false prophet.

Battle of the Burbs

By the end of 2014, the Takers completely devastated and raped the major cities. To survive they had to spread into the suburbs. They would not grow food since it required effort, which was foreign to their mental conditioning. Stolen supplies were being depleted. The stench of the inner city became too much for even a Taker. They started to tire of robbing, raping and killing each other. As with Army ants, once an area is picked clean, it was time to move.

The Producers trembled at the mere thought of the approaching enemy. They knew for some time this day, sooner or later would be here. Their scouts saw and smelled the advancing Taker hordes. All salvage vehicles and other debris was used to barricade all entry points into their community. The Takers Escalades started to run out of fuel as they approached the producer community. They now regretted wasting all that fuel on drive by shootings and joy riding. As their vehicles ran out of fuel, the men started the attack on foot, followed in the distance by the slower heavier women.

Thank God that the Obama Civilian Defense Force (OCDF) had just started confiscating the producer's weapons, before the end of the country. Obama's Civil Defense Force was dissolved when the countries economy collapsed. Even AmeriCorp volunteers left since they no longer were paid. The OCDF would never require the Takers to relinquish their illegally obtained and possessed weapons. This action would cost the Progressives needed votes, and perhaps the Takers and the New Black Panther Party could substitute someday for the OCDF. Obama will need armed and bloodthirsty thugs to do his bidding. This was now his only path to stay in power. His new nickname was Big Daddy B.O.

I remembered that when the government takes the weapons from honest, responsible citizens, the weapons remaining would be in the hands of the criminals. The crime rate decreased wherever Producers could defend themselves. The reason for this statistic was simple. If my person or property was threatened, premium hollow point rounds from my Smith and Wesson Air weight 38 revolver would ruin ones day.

The suburban Conservative Producers in the "Blue States" were prepared for the advancing Takers. The Producers stationed snipers in the tallest buildings, and fortified their positions. The Taker men opened fire. They were not fast enough to out run the producers bullets. This battle would not go the way of the large cities largely inhabited by Progressives. The Taker men were cut down in full stride. Their bodies littered the once well-manicured lawns. By the time the Taker women made it to the scene, the battle was largely over. A few Taker Women continued the fight, while many had to sit down and rest. The women who continued to fight were cut down by the producer gunfire. Those women still at rest had enough sense to flee the battle. One Taker Woman was overhead screaming, "It is better to run away and reproduce another day". This was a puzzling statement when heard by the producers. They were raised and taught with a different mindset.

The remaining Takers in the Blue Conservative States, after taking a "woo -pin" decided to bypass the suburban producer strongholds and go after the "hillbillies". Their knowledge of country people came from watching old reruns of "Dukes of Hazard" and "Green Acres".

In the "Red Progressive States" the suburban producers faired worse in battling the Takers. The Takers breached their fortifications with both sides taking heavy causalities. These Producers had fewer weapons to defend themselves. The battle at the end was hand to mouth combat. In this battle there were no winners. The dead bodies on each side were stacked like firewood, and burned on the spot. All the Takers who fought died or were wounded in the battle, and hardly enough producers survived to dispose of the bodies.

Country Boy's can Survive

Some Americans living in the deep woods and mountains of Alaska, Southeast and West did not notice the fall of the Federal Government. When they came back to civilization, they were shocked at the news. They bought whatever supplies left to purchase, and headed back to the wilderness. These people who had little need for cities, fared better than most during the economic collapse. Always well armed with a 30-30 rifle and a Colt 45 Pistol, they hunted game and raised a garden. Water came from a spring or well. It didn't matter if it had to be carried into the cabin. You had enough water for drinking, cooking and dishwashing. Not much water was wasted in bathing. Besides, you seldom came in contact with outsiders. Going to the restroom meant a well vented out house. Wealthy people had a two holed variety. My geologic knowledge says the outhouse should be down slope from the well or spring. The "privy" was made to be portable. Once the original pit was full, a new pit was dug and the privy was dragged to the new site. Young boys had the honor of digging the new pit and filling in the old one. After a heavy rain, never walk upon a filled pit. It forms a country boy's version of "quick sand". Progressive newspapers were recycled as toilet paper. They also were good for starting fires. Why else would a conservative buy that trash!

Every cabin had a well build stone fireplace. There was never a shortage of fuel. Country Boy's could run a trout line, make homemade wine. They loved to hunt and fish. How could that be thought as work? I could go fishing all day. If asked by my wife what I was doing, I could proudly say "Working". Momma can bake and cook from scratch, using whatever is at hand. Daddy can make "Shine". A famous quote from Sarah Palin "We eat therefore we hunt". Most Americans could not relate to this statement. Her remarks made in 2009 brought much ridicule from the liberal press and fellow Progressives. They constantly looked for any reason to belittle her. In 2013 she was the profound scholar of our time. Sarah was in great demand for her wisdom, charm and survival skills. Tina Fey facing starvation and pursued by the Takers, wished she were the real Sarah Palin, not some comical imitator. Her making fun of Sarah made Tina Fey the darling of NBC and the Progressives. She was showered with awards such as The Kennedy Center for the Performing Art's Mark Twain Prize for American Humor. Also in her trophy case was seven Emmys, three Golden Globes, four Screen actors Guild Awards and four Writers Guild of America Awards. This is proof that liberals dominate Hollywood and most other media. All this past acclaim and notoriety was now meaningless.

As she hid from the Takers, she thought back to the days when she was the center of attention at every New York dinner party. She wished for just one bite of that luxuriant food. Tina Fey wished now to be more like Sarah, instead of a weak, hapless liberal. In the past she never owned a gun. Tina wished now for a gun, so she could defend herself against the Takers. Being delirious, she dreamed she was Sarah Palin. Without food or water for many days, when the Takers found her emaciated dying body, they took pity and did not rape or kill her. At the end, her perceived by some humorous jabs at Sarah Palin was not a laughing matter.

People living in the wilderness can survive by hunting, gathering and fishing. This type of lifestyle depends on the land being sparsely populated. Otherwise you will over hunt or fish the native animals. Any intruder into their area will not be tolerated. In the year 2013, it will be shooting first and ask questions later. It might take a long time for the mounted police to arrive. At least the police will be forced to abandon their radar guns.

On my property in Tennessee there are wild turkeys, deer, squirrels, ducks, doves and rabbits. I love to watch these animals and would hate very much to eat them. Our roles will be reversed. We used to feed the wild animals, now they will feed my family. In the past I put out hundred of pounds of bird food, thistle seeds for the beautiful Golden Finches and corn for the deer and turkeys. One morning I wondered if the birds cared about the person who bought and placed before them his bounty of food. Did they take my efforts for granted? Was their only emotion sadness that I can no longer provide food?

In the year 2013, it will always be hunting season. The number of "road kill" will diminish due to the scarcity of vehicles on the road. Every recently deceased or nearly deceased carcass will be greatly contested. It was easier for wild animals to avoid being hit by a horse and buggy than a car. Progressives tried to protest their loss of governmental power by blocking a road in the supine position. Had they not heard of the "Road Kill Bill" in Tennessee? Note- when skinning and gutting a polecat, great caution should be used!

To be fair there is one drawback to country living - Chiggers. This larvae stage of mites, once on your person, causes great irritation. Chiggers are parasites that cling to and ingest your skin. I have never seen a good parasite, either insect or man. There is one advantage to residing in an asphalt and concrete jungle.

Country Livin will greatly increase my physical work load. I also will be in better health, lose weight and hopefully diabetes. Office work has never been the life for me.

My View of the World

Front Yard

Back Yard

My lovely oaks trees visually outline and frame my house. If Progressives and environmentalist destroy the economy, I will be forced to cut these trees to provide heat during the winter and fuel for cooking. The first trees to be surrendered will be the dead and dying oaks from wood ant infestation. Next will be the most painful, cutting down healthy trees. I would hate to burn wood for the following reasons:

1. I am lazy, cutting trees, stacking firewood; carrying it to the wood stove and removing the ashes are work.
2. It smokes up the outdoors. (Out side the house air pollution)
3. It smokes up the indoors. (In side the house air pollution)

Advantages of burning wood

1. Keeps you toasty on a cold winter's night
2. Pisses off the environmentalist
3. Nothing beats the smell, sound and sight of a tree part on fire.
4. Even without electricity, my wife will never have an excuse not to cook. I will keep her well supplied with wood for the cook stove.

Note to Environmentalist:

You should be pleased that I am creating less trash. I was sad that I could no longer purchase the products that would generate refuse. The large Styrofoam McDonalds coffee cup with steamy super hot contents will be missed. Now with the economy of a third world nation, survival takes precedence over the environment. All our efforts and thoughts are to obtain enough food to survive another day and to stay clear of violence.

My carbon footprint will go from a size twelve to ninety seven. Instead of my trash sent to a landfill, it will be burnt with the incombustibles buried in my ravine. The Takers will drop their load anywhere non-humanly possible.

To cook we will burn wood in the outside cook stove and over the inside fire place when the weather is cold. The fire place will serve dual purposes of cooking and heat. During the winter smoke from my fireplace will be

They were watching us, as we watched them. Who will be victorious?

seen and smelt for miles around. Burning tree parts will be a 24/7 operation. I am lucky to live in a rural area. If this is attempted by city dwellers, the air will be clogged with thick choking acrid smoke. City folks could go green and freeze. During the cold winter I wish there was global warming instead of being another environmental hoax! All the environmental gains for the last fifty years will be negated. If some Greenie doesn't like my air pollution, don't come on my property. It might be a time of shoot first and ask questions later. If you survive, I will make you watch a tree part on fire. For fun, I might make the greenie skin a pole cat. In the time to come, animals on the endangered list really will be endangered.

Environmental conditions worsen where the vultures were eating themselves. A similar thing happened to Lawyers (Joke). Humans were competitors for most of the remaining road kill and any other fresh carcass. We watched the vultures and they watched us. Do Vultures care if their food stinks? Maybe, since they fly around waiting for some animal to die. That way they can land and start gorging themselves at the moment of perfection. Vultures are ugly birds with baldheads. The absence of head and neck feathers is so they can get deep inside some dead animal while feeding and not soil their feathers. Who knew they cared about appearance? Their long broad wings are designed for long distance soaring. This energy saving technique of catching rising thermals is critical when slowly circling watching your food die.

Thank God I have a septic tank instead of a sewer. My septic system will not fail me like those on sewer systems. Sewers will become nothing more than a rat hotel. Even if you had water to flush your commode, the sewer system will be hopelessly clogged. It might even back up into your fancy penthouse, making quite a gooey nasty mess. A disadvantage of not having a sewer is eliminating a place to hide from the Takers and losing a prime rodent hunting ground. By 2014, the remaining Greenies tried to place rats on the endangered species list. I made my own list, placing Progressives and Greenies number one and two, respectively, closely followed by the rats. Water from my well will be hand carried to fill the tank on the toilet. The joy of sitting on the porcelain throne will always be mine. My new motto "add water and flush". At least this joy of life will always be mine. In many ways, my lifestyle is less affected than most. This will be my form of recycling.

On my five acres we will grow a garden, and raise several head of miniature Hereford cattle. These cattle are very "adorable" and a tear will be shed when they are slaughtered, butchered and consumed. It will be like eating a pet. We will also have free-range chickens. At night they will be locked securely in the chicken coop. This will keep other critters from eating my chickens. They will provide fresh eggs and in their older non-producing days, country fried chicken. I can almost taste the chicken fried in a cast iron skillet on the wood cook stove. Breakfast will be country ham, fresh eggs and biscuits made from scratch. My wife will insist that I light her fire! I am so old; I might have to rise early to accomplish this task. Without modern conveniences my wife will never be the same. These hard times will bring us closer as a family.

If people buy this book, I will build a fence around my property and stockpile food and supplies. Then I can follow the words of my mentor "Glenn Beck".

Takers Versus Country Boys

Any "Taker" or others that attempt to steal from wilderness and country folks, will have a rude awakening. The takers that made it this far pillaging, raping and plundering are showing significant signs of "Wear and Tear". Many wore all the stolen "bling" from earlier campaigns. If their trophies of war were not on their person, most definitely another taker would steal it. Many tried to bury or hide their stolen loot. This was a failure because after a few days, they forgot where it was hidden. Being exhausted from a long campaign and weighted down with pounds of 14-karat gold chains, even the male takers could no longer run. The Takers were easy to spot during the day. The sunrays glittered off their 14-karat gold, sterling silver jewelry and the multiple large diamond stud earrings that completely lined their ear lobes. During the day this reflection gave away their location. Even with near total darkness when the Takers were moving, you could hear the clanging of "Bling" and smacking of lips. A good well-trained dog could smell them from miles away. The Takers after learning about this always tried to attack staying up wind from the producers. When the dogs started barking, the producers knew it was time to lock and load. Since all coons and other wild animals were eaten years ago, there were few false alarms. Sadly only a few dogs and even fewer cats had survived.

Thousands of vultures were soaring above the scene of the impending battle. How did they know what was to occur?

The attack of the Takers against the country folks seemed to be in slow motion. The country folk loved to hunt and had plenty of guns and ammo. Both sides were well armed and motivated. The Takers wanted the local's food, weapons, and ammo, jewelry, gold and young women. The country folk were defending their homes and very existence. Takers were good at using handguns; country folks were expert hunters using Winchester 30-30 hunting rifles with long distance scopes. The Takers were dropped often without even seeing the shooter. The country boys thought it was open season. From this day forward, there was never a limit. You could bag as many Takers as were in the field. Being concealed and wearing their finest camouflage, the country boys were hidden from view. Only a few Takers came within range for the country boys to use handguns and even fewer for the use of shotguns firing 000 Buckshot. As mentioned earlier, the weapon of choice for up close fighting is the shotgun. With only a few casualties, the country boys had several excellent days of hunting. Some were a little sad when after three days of intense fighting the guns fell silent. It took several days for the euphoria to diminish. The end of the battle came at a good time, since the country boys were running low of 30-30 ammo and their rifle barrels were red-hot. The hot rifle barrels at night put off a warming glow, but could give up your location.

The French complained that the Country Boys did not use NATO approved ammunition. Since NATO was now extinct, the complaints by the French as always were irrelevant. The Country Boys would never capitulate to the Takers like the French or any other Progressive. Our civilian Federal Government defense policies in the past had made victory almost impossible. Thank God the country boys were freed to fight to win since the Federal Government had long dissolved.

All Takers who did retreat from the field of action were now dead are dying. Vultures were busy reading the menu. Seeing some of the Taker women brought a rare smile. The day after the battle there was a moment of silence at high noon observed through out the countryside. This silence was broken by the soothing sound of starting John Deere diesel engines. The dozers and tractors with front end loaders dug deep wide trenches in which to bury the dead. Extra deep and wide pits were excavated to deposit many of the Taker Women. The bodies were coated with lime and covered with fertile dark topsoil. Before burying the Takers, the country boys collected the "bling" and weapons from the bodies. This huge bounty of "bling" weighed in at 2.75 tons. This bounty was equally distributed to all the country boys. Those patriots who were seriously wounded and the families of the souls who died were given five times the portion that of the average defender.

Hostilities ceased on June 15, 2014. This being a new day of "Thanksgiving" was celebrated and always remembered in the country. The original Thanksgiving celebrated God blessings for a successful harvest and surviving harsh conditions. The country boys had a harvest of 14 kt gold, sterling silver and diamonds and had survived the second civil war. Most important they had the peace and freedom as ordained by God. Their families were safe, never again to be threatened by the Takers or "Others". They felt for the first time in many years that the worst was behind them.

Gold, silver and other precious metals replaced currency to facilitate the exchanging of goods. Locally a movement arose that any paper currency would be backed by precious metals. The icon of the left, Franklin Delano Roosevelt removed the U.S. off the gold standard in 1935. He also allowed deficit spending, higher taxes on the wealthy and increased regulation of banks and public utilities. The Progressive seeds of destruction were first sown many years ago.

The Aftermath

After the producers won the final battle with the Takers; all violence that existed was minor skirmishes. The people that survived, life was a daily struggle and they pondered the future. Government at every level was nonexistent. As in the beginning of our country, families looked to each other and God for support. If one wanted to eat, one must work! This was a new revelation for many.

If you had trouble walking, you could sew, cook or do dishes with assistance. Everyone was expected to contribute to the welfare of his or her family in anyway possible. Young boys would gather wood needed for the wood cook stove and carry wood needed to heat the home during the winter. Every fall after harvest, the men and boys cut, transported and stacked many loads of wood preparing for the chill of winter. Everyone worked in raising a garden. The women primarily did the canning along with cooking, cleaning and child rearing. The livestock had to be tended; hay was stored in the hayloft to feed the animals during the winter. Whole ears of corn were stored in silos for the kernels to harden. To survive, one must have planning, followed by hard work. Life was now much simpler without electricity. There were no cell phones, television, computers or electrical appliances (my wife was very sad). There was as in the old days, books to read. Many read the epic novel "The Next to Last American President" over and over again.

A remarkable thing occurred when many truly found Jesus for the first time. This included those who thought they were Christians. In important ways, life became less stressful. The Amish with their simpler way of living were in many ways happier and more content that the average American. Transportation choices consisted of walking or riding a horse or in a buggy. There were autos, but no gasoline. There was never a problem of having fat kids. Even I had slimmed down to a trim 220 pounds by the end of 2013. This weight loss eliminated the need for diabetes medication. This was timely since there was no medicine to be found.

Life began to improve with help and guidance from God. All people were forced to live a life like the Amish have for generations. You plowed the fields with horses or mules, grew crops and tended livestock. A diesel generator produced the limited needs for electricity. Water came from a well. The Amish were already disconnected from the grid for water and electricity, the loss of services was not greatly missed. Transportation was always by foot or buggy. If an Amish neighbor's house burnt, the community would come together and "Frolic" (rebuild the home). A similar event for rebuilding a barn was called "doing the job". The men would cut the trees, haul the logs to the site using horses and had a diesel powered generator to power the saw. The women folk would cook and provide the noontime meal. In many ways it was a spiritual community event that drew the people closer together. Everyone was expected to work, and help others as needed. How amazing this could be done without the hindrance of government?

The spirit and outlook of the people began to rebound. It started with individual family members, family to family, communities to communities. At harvest time there was a great surplus of food, which was shared with those who could not work. The distribution of food and all other public assistance was administrated through the Christian Churches, following the guidelines listed below:

1 Timothy 5-3-7 The church should take loving care of women whose husbands have died, if they don't have anyone else to help them. But if they have children or grandchildren, these are the ones who should take the responsibility, for kindness should begin at home, supporting needy parents. This is something that pleases God very much.

The church should care for the widows who are poor and alone in the world, if they are looking to God for his help and spending much time in prayer; but not if they are spending their time running around gossiping, seeking only pleasure and thus ruining their souls. This should be your church rule so that the Christians will know and do what is right.

As it is written, so shall it be done! One should never aid in destroying another's mortal soul! The people believed and followed exactly the word of God. They prospered and gave thanks on bended knees. Sundays were observed only as a day of worship.

Years ago Takers argued they had a right for social justice because of "Christian Charity". It is obvious that never read 1 Timothy chapter 5, verses 3-7. Most of the Takers would not quality for assistance. Thankfully only a few Takers remained in the new era.

A great spiritual and cultural revival sprung up, and spread throughout the land. Limited local government began in the small clusters. The people now realized that a more powerful government meant yielding of personal rights and responsibilities. Many for the first time in years "were proud of their country".

The boundaries of the former states were honored. All the old Progressive Politicians and their ways of thinking were now in the ash heap of history. Never again would the people yield their god given rights to any politician. Past political leaders such as Harry Reid and Nancy Pelosi thought the people existed to serve them and the government. Progressives like Barrack Obama deemed themselves superior in every way and knew what was best for the teeming masses. It did not matter what the people thought, as with Universal Health Care. Progressive Elites thought average man or woman not equal to them in wisdom or intelligence, and needed their guidance through government to chart their path in life.

Luke 10:21 Then he was filled with the joy of the holy spirit and said, "I praise your, O Father, Lord of heaven and earth, for hiding these things from the intellectuals and worldly wise and for revealing to those who are as trusting as little children.

Man must lower his eyes to see the brilliance of the lord. There can be only one spiritual godly master and we who believe his earthly servants. A vessel full of the pride of man lacks room for the mercy and wisdom of God. The meaning of life on earth is preparation for eternal salvation.

Liberty and freedom as given by God exist in a precious finite amount. The more of this godly gift, ceased by government meant less for the people. We would never allow this theft of rights in the future. This holy right must be defended at all cost. If not everlasting diligent, government in the pretense of doing good and its all-knowing politicians will slowly bit by bit steal your freedom, wealth and liberty. Progressives will turn your vision and thoughts away from the true and only God. To them, there is no god other than the all knowing, all seeing Federal Government!

The memories of the ultimate betrayal by government leading to fall of America in 2013 will always be firmly etched in the minds of the survivors and their children's children. Every history course in the future will teach this blasphemy, so that no one will forget!

Children will at first be home schooled. Later as with the Amish, small local community schools will be built. With no fuel for the leftover busses, schools must be close enough for the children to walk or ride in a horse drawn buggy. The schools for air conditioning had windows that would open. During the winter a potbelly cast iron wood stove provided heat. The fathers of the school children supplied the well season oak firewood. One older boy in the class was responsible for maintaining the stove, arriving an hour before class to start the fire. The teacher was paid in foodstuffs and with 14 karat gold jewelry. A free apartment was provided adjacent to the school. All the children would pack a hearty lunch prepared by their moms. Gone were the days of government paid breakfast, lunch and dinner for school children.

For religious producers, most churches were now too distant. People met in local homes, buildings, almost anywhere to worship the almighty God. One of my favorite verses:

Matthew 18:20 for where two or three are gathered together in my name, there am I in the midst of them.

Today's children were much different than before the crash. They are polite, honest, and taught to work, be responsible and to honor and respect their parents. Children scoffed at the morality and thinking of the Takers. A loving God-fearing married mother and father raised the children. No longer would "Uncle Sam" take the financial place of the father. The Federal Government lacked the moral authority to govern, much less be a parent.

Malachi 4-15 You were united to your wife by the Lord. In god's wise plan, when you married, the two of you became one person in his sight. And what does he want? Godly children from your union. Therefore guard your passions! Keep faith with the wife of your youth.

Out of wedlock births became almost non-existent, along with abortions. There was a rebirth of traditional family values and the belief in God. Most people, even the intellectuals gained wisdom.

Proverbs 4: 13-18 The man who know right from wrong and has good judgment and common sense is happier than the man who is immensely rich! For such wisdom is far more valuable than precious jewels. Nothing else compare with it. Wisdom gives: A long, good life   Riches   Honor   Pleasure   Peace.   Wisdom is a tree of life to those who eat her fruit; happy is the man who keeps on eating it.   Amen Brother

The Takers and the Progressive Movement was a dark chapter of history. Actually it was not their history, since for many the country started anew in 2014. The Lord was pleased with man in our former country for the first time in many years. AMEN

The United States was a remnant of the past. The Chinese occupied and controlled Alaska. La Raza and other Mexican Revolutionary Groups, along with help from the Mexican Army, reclaimed the "stolen territory" of California. The Mexican takeover was planned many years ago. Millions of Mexicans illegally crossed the U.S. Border to lie dormant awaiting the signal from La Raza. When the word was given to attack, the Illegal's greatly outnumber the "Gringos" and the native Hispanics, many who were Progressives. The Illegal's in California with aid from the Mexican Army and drug cartels forced the Californians to quickly surrender. Mexican Drug Cartels were upset with Americans for destroying the value of the currency, and hindering their illegal sale of drugs. Their millions in U.S. hundred dollars bills were now worthless. How could they sell their drugs without the dollar being a medium of exchange? Their customers could not even use their EBT cards. The natives of California without weapons had little means of defense. One benefit to the dope heads in California was growing; selling and smoking marijuana was now legal, free of interference from the Federal Government. Some never noticed or cared about California now being a Mexican Province. The addicts stayed in a drug-induced euphoria. The only good part of this story is that they live in another country.

President Romney strongly protested the takeover of California. Everyone knew the last President of the United States had no real power. Many Latinos in America whether legal or not, had a great celebration. In California the American Flag was lowered and replaced with the Mexican. This action was accompanied by the music of a mariachi band. Woman did a Mexican Hat Dance around the soiled American Flag, lying in the dirt near the base of the flagpole. After much jubilation and consumption of Tequila, a few drunken young well-endowed senoritas began to pole dance. A flagpole had never been used in that manner! The National Council of La Raza now governed the former state. Ronald Reagan's body had to removed and reburied in the State of Georgia at the base of Stone Mountain. His new burial site became an everlasting shrine to many Conservatives.

The National Council of La Raza and Mexican Government then attempted to take over Texas, Arizona and New Mexico. Illegal immigrant fighters and the Mexican Army met no resistance as normal crossing the southern border with Arizona. The Federal Government under both Republican and Democratic Presidents were never serious about defending our southern border. The La Raza General, El Stinky, made a strategic military blunder believing the citizens of Texas, Arizona and New Mexico would easily capitulate like the Californians. The "Gringos" of the three states successfully counter attacked the Mexicans during their siesta, catching them completely off guard. La Raza and the Mexican Soldiers were defeated in a major battle near Phoenix and were forced to retreat back to Mexico and California. They left behind a trail of half eaten tortillas. La Raza and the Mexican Government sued for peace. Texas, Arizona and New Mexico signed a peace treaty with La Raza and Mexico. The borders would stay as before and the three States settled for the Mexicans to stay in Mexico and they could keep California. Mexico would order all the illegal immigrants home and promised never to invade US again.

The Muslims were elated that Barrack helped to destroy the "Great Satan". One unexpected outcome was all the billions of US Currency held by the Saudis and other Muslim's were now worthless. With the collapse of the world's economy, so did the demand for their oil. Things did not work out exactly as planned. Without foreign Muslim terrorist financial support, the mosque built near "Ground Zero" in New York City went into foreclosure. It was later turned into a strip joint.

Former President Obama, snug in his Chicago Mansion, knew his revenge on America was complete, found his old prayer rug and gave thanks to Allah! He made one last trip to Saudi Arabia where he was given a medal for being a Muslim in the highest standing and for his continual support of Islam. He had destroyed the "Great Satan" and lived to tell about it.

Barry was now despised is his old country, but a super star in the Muslim World. He and his New Muslim Black Panther Party Bodyguards flew to Saudi Arabia. When meeting the Saudi King to receive another medal, he again bowed deeply from the waist and kissed the left hand of the King. The King's other hand was used only for wiping. This became more of an issue with the shortage of toilet paper and hand soap.

He again apologized for the past arrogance of America. The Saudi King was not interested in hearing this story again. Barrack finally arose and the King placed the medal around his neck. This thick heavy 24K gold chain and medallion was Obama's second King Abdul Aziz Order of Merit Award. The Muslims were elated that Barrack helped to destroy the "Great Satan". One unexpected outcome was all the billions of US Currency held by the Saudis and other Muslim's were now worthless. With the collapse of the world's economy, so did the demand for their oil. Things did not work out exactly as planned.

The boys of the hood were envious of his "Bling". He wore both medals proudly at the next convention of the National Association for the Advancement of Liberal Colored People. (NAALCP), His keynote speech at the convention was a glittering event. All who watched and listened were dazzled. As always, it did not matter to his supporters that his words were utter nonsense. After all, he was a historical footnote in history. Convention attendance was down, since the attendees had to pay their own way and there would be no coverage on television. Some gullible people still believed in the "One".

In the conservative areas of the former country, there was a "Don't Ask, Don't Tell Policy". Those of this life choice that remained in these areas missed the "Gay Ole Times". There was a mass migration west by wagon trains to their city, San Francisco. This sin city had similar phrases as Las Vegas. "What you want, when you want it! My favorite was "What happens in San Fran, Stays in San Fran". Many homosexual migrants after weeks of travel arrive in San Francisco only to learn that California was now a Mexican Province.

A week after hearing this disheartening news, San Francisco and other major west coast cities were evaporated by Chinese nukes. The Chinese investment in Bill Clinton really paid off.! As a professional courtesy, the Chinese Premier gave Clinton advance notice of twenty-four hours to leave town. The only stipulation given to Clinton is that he could not tell or take anyone, not even Hillary. Bill protested and the Chinese soften their stance. Mr. Clinton and Chelsea took the last flight that afternoon to Beijing.

Louis Farrakhan, Jeremiah Wright and other Black Liberationist still looked for the "Promise Land." Now with the destruction of America, they lacked a country or race to hate or blame for their shortcomings. Fortunately for them, there still were plenty of white people to hate. The racial pimps had already closed up shop. There were no media or microphones, no money or fame left in the racial pimping business.

The New State Conferences of America

The United States of America was no more, going the way of the old Soviet Union. The states left of the once great country formed new associations due to similar geography, culture, language, religion and college sports. These conferences formed on May 26, 2015.

The remaining states formed regional associations. The grouping of states is as follows:

South East Conference of States (SEC -OS) - Tennessee, Georgia, Kentucky, Alabama, Virginia, South Carolina, Florida, Mississippi, Texas, Arkansas, North Carolina, Louisiana and West Virginia. We had to keep all the South Eastern Conference (SEC) College Football and Basketball schools together, plus add other teams. The new SEC was enlarged and improved. I always had a warm spot in my heart for Texans. North Carolina was allowed entry only after dropping the lawsuit against Tennessee Valley Authority (TVA).

North East Conference of States (NEC-OS) - New York, Indiana, Iowa, Maryland, Minnesota, Massachusetts, Ohio, Pennsylvania, Rhode Island and Vermont, Maine, New Hampshire, Connecticut, New Jersey, Illinois, Delaware, Michigan, Minnesota, Wisconsin

Central Plains Conference of States (CPC-OS)- Idaho, Arizona, Missouri, Montana, Nebraska, Nevada, Utah, Wyoming, Oklahoma, Colorado, Kansas, New Mexico, North Dakota, South Dakota

West and Far West Conference (WAFWC-OS) - Hawaii, Washington, Oregon

Each geographic grouping of states held no power other than inside their boundaries. Each section of the country formed separate constitutions. Federal Governments would never have the power or control that led to the destruction of America. Many in the past, thought the United States of America was "too big to fail". Almost all of the former surviving Progressive National Politicians, whose decadent philosophy contributed to the destruction of America way of life, resided in a different country. Never again will their evil ideology be heard or tolerated. The conferences became sovereign countries with individual Constitutions. Stated below is the constitution of the SEC OS.

Constitution Of The Southeastern Conference of States

When in the Course of human events, it becomes necessary for one people to dissolve the political bonds, which have connected them with another, and to assume liberty and freedom as ordained from God. This action of separating from the United States of America was not done lightly; we were left with no recourse. We did not leave the United States of America, the United States of America left us many years ago. The prior government corrupted the people, creating a foundation of moral and financial infidelity. Immoral actions against God and Man would not stand! This erosion of values and the rule of law undermined the bedrock of the constitution leading to the downfall as the Soviet Union.

This constitution shall in no other ways infringe upon the rights of the States, or alter their existing laws or regulations.

We hold these truths to be self-evident, that the Creator with certain unalienable Rights created all men equal. God has endowed us with many rights. Among these are Life, Liberty, and the pursuit of Happiness. This constitution does not guarantee equal outcome, only freedom and lack of governmental interference to allow the human spirit to flourish. The Powers of the Conference Government shall always be limited. There exists only a finite amount of precious Liberty as granted by God. The more Liberty taken by government, less remains for mankind. The government understands it role in God's Holy Plan. Always number one in importance is God, followed by family, neighbors and Government.

All able-bodied men and women of sound mind and character must process Weapons and Ammunition needed for their personal protection and to aid and defend the freedoms of their State or SEC-OS by Foreign Aggressors. These Weapons must be of the semi-automatic variety up to fifty Calibers. You must at all times maintain at least one thousand rounds of ammunition for each weapon. If a citizen cannot afford this requirement, it shall be proved by the state after a complete moral, physiological and criminal background check. All children born into the SEC OS will be granted a lifetime membership in the New National Rifle Association (NNRA)
Each Member State must have a well trained and supplied National Guard. These part time soldiers must equal one percent of each States Population. Funding for each States National Guard is to be equally financially supported by the state and conference Governments. The headquarters of this civilian government and military Leadership shall be located in Montgomery, Alabama. This National Guard and civilians when called upon must defend and protect their State and collectively the Conference. War will always be the last resort. If this evil is forced upon us, we will use all means to end the hostility and bring our soldiers home victorious. We will not be afraid to call our enemies by name, and use all our power to defeat them. We shall not feminize our soldiers and the armed forces shall consist only of males who are real men. The purposes of the armed forces are to protect the borders and defend the homeland. The military is not a place for equal opportunity, social promotion or political correctness. Every soldier will first have allegiance to the one and true God, family and the SEC-OS. Any soldier not willing to fulfill this oath will be promptly removed.

We shall attempt to limit civilian casualties of the enemy, but this action in no way shall hinder our victory. The civilian government will declare war and then transfer the decisions of operational strategy to the military. The Council of War shall consist of a commanding general and one military advisor from each member state. The Council of War members shall be skilled, trained and competent to lead any war effort in defense of the homeland. A Conference Military College will be established in Montgomery, Alabama. Each member state will have one college dedicated to the history, strategies and mechanics of war. These colleges will train the officers of the National Guard, who will be our future leaders of the military. Our Military leaders will be modeled after General George S. Patton, Jr. He is regarded as one of the most successful field commanders of any war. There existed an unyielding man of extreme determination committed to victory. He was a true leader of men!

"If a man has done his best, what else is there? I don't measure a man's success by how high he climbs but how high he bounces when he hits bottom." - George S. Patton, Jr.

The sole function of this constitution is for all times; limit the power of the government. The limited powers of this Conference Government is national defense, border security, trade and as a fair and unbiased arbitrator of disputes between member States. All other powers remain with the member States and citizens. There shall be no unauthorized immigration to the Conference States. An impenetrable barrier will be built to protect and defend the southern border of Texas with Mexico and the state's western borders. Without borders there can be no country. Inner peace cannot exist with foreign interlopers. Any person living outside the conference wishing entry must be carefully scrutinized. Any foreigner admitted entry into the conference must be registered and monitored. These Aliens must demonstrate being of the highest moral character, without a documented criminal past. They must have some ability or skill that will contribute to society. Any child born in the conference is not considered a citizen unless one documented biological parent is also a citizen. We will otherwise adopt similar immigration policy as the Government of Mexico.

No one or entity outside the conference shall not contribute money or directly or indirectly support political candidates in the conference. This outside influence shall be promptly reported to the Conference Board of Ethics. Non conference news or political opinion shall be prohibited. CNN must relocate to the North Eastern Conference. The old line media that were the propaganda wing of the Progressives are not permitted in the South Eastern Conference of States. They had a decisive role in the destruction of the former country by being the propaganda wing of the Left.

The citizens of the SEC OS of sound mind and character over eighteen years of age shall through free and honest elections vote for their local, state and conference officials. The elections will be held every four years. The Conference Leadership will be in order of power are Chief Executive, Executive, Citizen and Representatives. The electorate will vote for one Chief Executive who will be the commander and chief. The Chief Executive will appoint the Executive to be the second in command. In such times the Chief Executive's cannot perform their duties due to death or severe illness, the Executive will become Chief Executive. There will be two Citizens elected from each State. For every five hundred thousand of each states population, that shall elect one representative to serve in the conference government. The Citizens and Representatives are equal branches of government. These political bodies write legislation and vote to enact it into law. The Chief Executive has the right to make line item vetoes of any bill. His will can be over ruled by a sixty percent majority of votes by the Citizens or Representatives.

There shall be freedom of religion. Anyone shall be permitted to worship as allowed by there conscious. It is proclaimed that all wisdom, freedom and liberty are gifts by the almighty, never to be infringed by man.

There shall be freedom of speech and that of the press. No one shall bear false witness against another. The free press shall never be in collusion with any individual, company or political party. They should be honest observers and reporters of events.

The South Eastern Conference of States (SEC OS) is authorized by its member states and people to print currency, which will be "Legal Tender" for all debts, public and private. This currency and coinage will always be backed by an equivalent value of gold, silver or platinum and never only the full faith and trust of Government. The Conference Government must never operate with deficit spending. The only exception would be when the Leaders of the Conference declare war on another country. All military means necessary must be taken to defend the member states and the conference. There shall be no substitute for victory. The deficit must be totally repaid within five years after the end of hostilities. The Valued added Tax rate temporary would be increased to accomplish this goal. Once the "War Loans" are repaid, this increased taxation will be removed.

Each coastal state that borders the Atlantic Ocean or the Gulf of Mexico shall have full rights of ownership and benefit of the areas from their coastline to ten miles offshore. This includes all recreational, cultural, and use of natural resources. The SEC OS will own and control all other offshore areas from ten to two hundred miles offshore. Revenues from the Conference Oceanic Areas shall be used to fund the Conference Government to benefit all people in the country. A national 5 percent Valued Added Tax (VAT) will be enacted to support the financial needs of the Conference.

The majority of the citizens of the member states ratified this constitution on August 12, 2015. The People then on bended knees gave thanks to God.

Rebirth of Capitalism

A group of patriots, one being Glen Beck, started a movement to restart Capitalism. Glen gave his full attention to this matter, since at first there was no television, radio or books to write. They formed a new monetary system, where all paper currency would be backed by gold. This would be the new gold standard. Glen is one of the few former American's who "had enough gold to need a shovel". Instead of dollars, the method of trade would be the point system. An ounce of gold initially would be worth 1200 points. You knew that the currency always held value, since it was fully backed by gold, silver or other precious metals. The conference government would strictly control printing of paper currency to uphold its value and acceptance.

The Free Enterprise System was reborn with a means to conduct trade. Paper money would always be backed by something of value. No longer will the Federal Government be able to print money that one day would be worthless. All prices of goods and services were in points, not dollars. People will never again accept currency of the former United States. A loaf of bread initially was 4.3 points, 6.29 points for a gallon of milk. The faith in the monetary system slowly returned to pre-Obama levels. Each Conference of States had their separate and distinct currency.

Never again would one region of the former country dominate another either politically or economically. Until the national elections of November 2010, we were ruled by a bunch of "Chicago Thugs", the San Francisco Princess, Nancy Pelosi and dirty Harry Reed of Nevada. Thank God that in the year of 2015, these people do not reside in my country. Extra strength Pine Sol was needed to remove their filth and stench from society. Politicians in other conferences had no control or influence over another. The conferences are to remain separate and distinct countries to the end of time.

Companies now had a means to be compensated for the goods they produced and services provided. They had hope and certainty that government will not strangle their ambitions or steal the fruits of their labor. The public again had confidence in their Government and its currency. The economy rebounded, and millions of jobs were created. All monetary transactions were in the point system. The free enterprise system operated more efficiently then in the past. Many unnecessary taxes and regulations were never reinstated. The sound of prosperity filled the land. You could hear and see the engine of economic activity roar back to life. People and business had freedom to fulfill their highest ambitions. This was as envisioned by the founding fathers. As never seen before, citizens in our conference of states became a shining beacon of light that illumined the path for all to follow. Europe and the rest of the world were coming out of the economic dark ages. Many looked and emulated the work and thinking of the Southeastern Conference of States.

Only a few hard core Progressive missed the old Federal Government. Some in essence had lost their only purpose in life. They no longer worshiped the heathen monuments of the institution of government. Nature was protected and loved by all, but never again worshipped as a "God". Al Gore was released early from prison for boring behavior on April Fools Day, April 1, 2015. The other inmates could not take the "stiff" one day longer. He spent the rest of his days, silently and without motion staring at a hackberry tree in his back yard. He would never molest another masseuse.

The Conference States of America particularity in the South Eastern Conference would never permit unions. They knew union bosses in the past, had hindered job creation and made products and services more expensive. These union bosses were in league with the progressives, socialist and communists. They cared not about their actions against humanity, only power and wealth. One should be careful with who you embed. Inefficiencies of the old system had to be excised like a cancer. Never again would the people allow the creation of the "Entitlement State." The newly elected political leaders would only have limited powers over the people. The Southeastern Conference of States and all others who followed their path had a golden age of peace and human advancement. The motto inscribed on many monuments and written in every textbook was: WE EAT, THEREFORE WE WORK!

The people that remained into late 2015 were nothing like their secular counter parts of 2010. Many Progressives in the past denied the existence of the one true God and instead worshiped themselves, nature and the power of the almighty government. These Progressives went the way of the old Federal Government. Most of the people who survived were honest, hardworking, self-reliant and god fearing. We had a "don't ask, don't tell" policy towards Progressives.

The survivors believed in less government, taxation and regulation. The only history taught of the prior "Dark Ages" that ended in 2014, was how the Progressives lack of family values, high taxation and reckless spending to appease their constituents had destroyed the former United States of America. This history was never to be repeated!

In this new age, people cared less about material things. They were content and pleased with their lives leaving behind many of the social and cultural challenges of the past. People never desired the latest gadget, Windows 29 Upgrade, or the 2015 version of the Apple I Pad. The most important items were God, Family and inner peace.

In some ways the people almost thanked the prior regime, since out of the ashes of the old United States blossomed a new era of enlightenment. God looked down from heaven and was pleased. The people finally realized that obeying and following the word of God, brought true happiness on Earth and everlasting joy in heaven. Everyone who was able worked. Families and communities took care of their own with out governmental assistance. Those who were old enough remembered how in the name of social justice, the tentacles of government attached and ruined the heart and morals of the people. The church supported the truly needy Christians, without family. This is how the apostle Paul wrote it. What advice given by the one true God is ever wrong? Thank God all immediate family survived the chaos and are healthy and happy. Two of my grown sons still live with my wife and me. Some things never change!

Early 2014, Kroger's and many closed businesses began to reopen. At first they sold only basic essential items such as bread, milk, meat, flour, rice and Hershey's Dark Chocolate Bars in the 3.52-ounce size. By late 2015 they offered a wide selection of products, but never the same variety as before. Who needs 35 varieties of breakfast cereal? They later sold flowers, toys and 25 varieties of ice cream.

Police, fire and other essential services began to function. Police and fire fighters were now cross-trained to perform both jobs. This saved money and made the government more efficient. Government employees were no longer controlled by the unions.

With electricity, water, Internet service and a plentiful supply of fuel, I had no excuse but to go back to work. Like most of the country, I had to start over. It took five long years of work to grow my income to an equivalent level as 2010. When electricity returned to my home, the washing machine and television spontaneously started. You would not believe this, but the television channel was still set to Fox. My wife was so overjoyed that a tear of happiness was shed. She was also thrilled with the return of air conditioning, knowing she would never have to fan me on hot humid summer nights. I will miss the peace and quiet, with sounds made only from the birds and other creatures in nature, one being my wife.

Direct TV re organized and launched new satellites into orbit. In the new country Fox once again was the dominant cable channel. All my favorite shows are back on the air. Glen Beck, Bill O'Reilly and Shawn Hannity looked and sounded better than ever. Their shows were more enjoyable without the tainted words from their Progressive Guests. Glen Beck was now honored for his investigative work exposing and informing the public years ago of the impending political and economic downturn. He received the Pulitzer Prize, Chancellor Award and the Tobenkin Award.

Further encouraging economic signs was the re grand opening of McDonalds. With such anticipation I barely slept the prior night. Awaking at 4 AM the opening day, I waited for an hour parked at the drive thru speaker waiting for the store to open. When all at once a voice was heard over the speaker "Welcome to McDonalds, how can I help you". I was overtaken with emotion but took time to gather myself and said: "I would like a large coffee, two creams, five equals on the side, Sausage McMuffin and a small ice water." The cashier replied it would be 4.35 points and I pulled around to pay the cashier. After receiving my tasty delights, I flew back to my new office to sample my treasures. The coffee was warm and enticing, the sausage mcmuffin melted in my mouth. This was my first purchase with my new debit card since the bank reopened. I knew at that moment, that everything would be ok.

Those who listened and followed the words of Mr. Beck prospered better than the general population. The companies who advertised on The Glen Beck Show were thanked for encouraging listeners to buy gold, survival food and non-hybrid seeds enough to grow a one-acre survival garden. Rush Limbaugh, Mark Levine and Shawn Hannity were back on the radio. Sadly most of the progressive radio and television programs never returned. These programs had poor ratings even before the crash.

The banking and monetary system was restored, but there was no longer a bank on every corner. All the old currency was ordered shredded. This brought a tear to an old bank manager. After all, it was just paper! The paper was recycled to make toilet paper. US coinage was melted down and made into new appliances and autos. My once favorite bank teller "Angie" was rehired and resumed her former position at the drive thru window.

Other improvements in the new country were that the court system was never "supreme". That designation was only reserved for "God". All judges both at the state and conference level will strictly follow the word and intent of their respective constitutions. No judge at any level will have a lifetime appointment. Judges in the future valued their pledge to uphold and defend the meaning and intent of the SEC-OS constitution.

Most radical liberal professors did not survive the end of America. They lived in large cities and would never own a weapon. Their supposed intellectual superiority proved to be of little benefit when the Takers came for them. Students would never have their hearts and minds tainted by the words of Rabid Progressives.

People of all races, ages and religious beliefs lived together in harmony. No one carried over to the new age, racial resentment or bigotry. Reparations were again paid in blood. The Progressive and Black Liberation thinking were absence in the houses of God. All true Christians placed "Christ" first and only in their hearts and minds. It was told that some of the Black Liberations like Louis Farrakhan and Jeremiah Wright were still looking for the Promised Land. Jessie Jackson and Al Sharpton stayed retired to be found on their front porch rocking chairs. Thanks god, I live in a different country. The dream of Martin Luther King was finally realized. Maybe this was now the "Promised Land". This reminds me that many were still waiting for the first coming of Christ. They apparently missed that he was here two thousand years ago.

Automakers began to hire and produce new vehicles. The South became prosperous without the unions, progressives, crime and despair. The factories and workers had lain dormant for too long. Every company that existed in 2014 was a mere shell of its former self. Only Ford Motor Company of the former "Big and Little Three" automakers had survived. The billions of dollars wasted for the auto union bailout of General Motor and Chrysler, turned out to be an expensive temporary union job program. Obama's union bailout's of GM (Government Motors) and Chrysler was another step in the destruction of the former country. This act of appeasement was to placate the political base and hell with the rest of the country.

With a booming economy factories worked around the clock to meet pent up demand. Every person who desired a job, found one. Those who could work but chose not, voluntarily went hungry. These people were given one way passage to their country of choice.

California was now a Mexican Province and the Chinese occupied the former federal lands in Alaska. Countless more millions of poor souls perished when the Chinese nuked the major cities along the West coast. These annihilated cities would be uninhabitable for many years. The few remaining environmentalist were pleased that nature would reclaim these cities among the bones and ashes of the deceased.

The states and conferences assumed all military equipment and supplies that were in their domain under the old Federal Government. Various conferences traded among each other to supply their State Guard Units.

The military needs of each conference of states were minimal. Never again would we fight a war on foreign soil. If attacked by a foreign entity, we will respond with massive air strikes. There will be no "Nation Building" only annihilation of our enemies. The SEC-OS built and maintained a modern nuclear deterrent. Each State had separate Guard Units under its control. In case of war the states would combine their Guard units under a conference commander. The United States Military of old was a vestige of the former country. Past members of the military unless adsorbed into the new State Guard units were now civilians. All progressive past military leaders of the old country would never again be "Leaders of Men!"

The new Conference of States did not honor the former federal government's laws or past financial obligations. This limited new government did not create the problems of old, and lacked tax revenue or other resources to repay this debt. This meant that most pension, retirement, health care or entitlement programs were null and void. This loss for many was a harsh reminder of the olds days. Gone were military, business, government and many individual pension plans. Unless one heeded the advice of Glen Beck and other conservatives to buy gold, your retirement outlook was bleak. Any investment or retirement plan that was based on the dollar was worthless. Taxes in the new era were minimal since there was no "Nanny State". Local taxes to fund education, police and fire and other services came from property taxes and a four percent sales tax. Taxation at the state level consisted of another four percent. The SEC OS Government levied a four percent Value Added Tax.

Health care industry began to rebound. Most doctors, nurses and other medical staff returned to work. Hospitals and pharmacies began to operate. The idea of many receiving free medical care was no more. People became prudent consumers of health care as every other product or service. Private companies offered only catastrophic health coverage. There was a tax-deductible health savings plan, with a twenty-five hundred-point deductible. Once the funds in their health savings account reached their deductible amount, excess monies could be spent or applied to pay future premiums. Health insurance premiums were reasonable due to the reduction in the cost of providing care. There would be no need for expensive malpractice insurance. An honest, unbiased arbitrator settled medical Malpractice claims. This eliminated the wasteful need for doctors to perform "defensive medicine." No longer would the government require hospitals to provide care for free or at a greatly reduced cost. In olden days, hospitals and other medical providers charged those with private health coverage extra to cover cost shifting from the government and mandated charity care. The old Federal Government expected medical services to be provided regardless of cost and whether payment was made.

People went back to work in every state conference. Food was inexpensive and plentiful. Standards of living seem to improve daily. One sad note is that eighty nine million six hundred and forty five thousand people, both legal and illegal residents perished from the end of the old country to the "Rebirth". Many died due to disease, famine or violence. Most of the Takers did not survive. The remaining few were forced into a different way of life. Many of the remaining illegal immigrants fled to California or Mexico. Conditions now were very different, but in many ways for the better. Mankind started to move towards a new era of enlightenment. Maybe we had found the "Promised Land."

www.ingramcontent.com/pod-product-compliance
Lightning Source LLC
Chambersburg PA
CBHW020442290526
45785CB00002B/974